Praise for *How Women Help Men Find God*

"Brilliant. Absolutely brilliant. And humorous and engaging and ever so insightful. David Murrow's wit and wisdom make for a terrific combination. Even better, Murrow offers practical help for women and churches to bring men to God. It's perhaps the most comprehensive and sensible book of its kind."

Marcia Ford
Journalist and Author, *We the Purple: Faith, Politics, and the Independent Voter*

"Just when I thought nothing could top his last best-selling book, David Murrow has penned another masterpiece! With cut-to-the-chase insights into the hearts and minds of men, along with fun doses of edgy wit, this groundbreaking resource is sure to revolutionize the spiritual impact women (and churches) have on men. Want to know how to jump start a man's spiritual engine? The tools you'll need are within these pages."

Ginger Plowman
Author, *Don't Make Me Count to Three* and *Heaven at Home*

"David Murrow lets women in on the secrets of a man's soul. An original, strategic thinker, Murrow's book will change the way we do church."

Rebekah Montgomery
Editor, *Right to the Heart of Women*

"Aha! Dave Murrow confirms what I have thought all along—men and women are different. As such, they approach matters of faith differently. For any woman who loves a man who doesn't share her same commitment to Christ, *How Women Help Men Find God* is a must-read. Not only does Murrow show women why our tactics, plans, and ploys to get our men to church more often than not blow up in our faces, he also suggests better ways to support and encourage these men whom we so desperately want to join us in the faith."

Nancy Kennedy
Author, *When He Doesn't Believe*

"David's conversational, big-brother-sitting-across-the-kitchen-table style of writing begs the book be read in one sitting. I had to force myself to slow down so I could savor each chapter, turning the truths over and over in my mind. Questions and an action item at each chapter's end deliver practical, I-can-do-this-right-now ideas for application."

Nancy Sebastian Meyer
Author, *Beyond Expectations* and *Spiritually Single Moms*

"The church is about both genders being fully present, engaged and redeemed for God's kingdom work. This book may make you uncomfortable at times but the points it makes are worthy of consideration."

Elisa Morgan
CEO, MOPS International
Publisher, *FullFill*

"David Murrow is thought-provoking, engaging, and convincing. He makes a strong case that if there is to be a faith revival among men, it's up to women to start it. This is a call to arms—and a challenge I know today's women are up to."

Mary Byers
Author, *How to Say No…and Live to Tell About It*

HOW WOMEN
HELP MEN
FIND GOD

DAVID MURROW

THOMAS NELSON
Since 1798

NASHVILLE   DALLAS   MEXICO CITY   RIO DE JANEIRO   BEIJING

How Women Help Men Find God
© 2008 by David Murrow

Published in Nashville, Tennessee, by Thomas Nelson. Thomas Nelson is a registered trademark of Thomas Nelson, Inc.

Published in association with WordServe Literary, 10152 Knoll Circle, Highlands Ranch, CO 80130, www.wordserveliterary.com.

Thomas Nelson, Inc., titles may be purchased in bulk for educational, business, fund-raising, or sales promotional use. For information, please e-mail SpecialMarkets@ThomasNelson.com.

Unless otherwise noted, Scripture quotations are taken from the NEW KING JAMES VERSION. © 1982 by Thomas Nelson, Inc. Used by permission. All rights reserved.

Scripture quotations marked NIV are from the Holy Bible: New International Version®. © 1973, 1978, 1984 by International Bible Society.
Used by permission of Zondervan Publishing House. All rights reserved.

Scripture quotations marked NASB are from the NEW AMERICAN STANDARD BIBLE®, © The Lockman Foundation 1960, 1962, 1963, 1968, 1971, 1972, 1973, 1975, 1977, 1995. Used by permission.

Scripture quotations marked NLT are from the *Holy Bible*, New Living Translation. © 1996, 2004 by Tyndale Charitable Trust. Used by permission of Tyndale House Publishers, Inc., Wheaton, Illinois 60189. All rights reserved.

Scripture quotations marked CEV are from THE CONTEMPORARY ENGLISH VERSION. © 1991 by the American Bible Society. Used by permission.

Library of Congress Cataloging-in-Publication Data

Murrow, David.
    How women help men find God / David Murrow.
        p. cm.
    Includes bibliographical references.
    ISBN 978-0-7852-2632-1 (pbk.)
    1. Christian men—Religious life. 2. Church work with men. I. Title.
BV639.M4M66 2008
248.8'42—dc22
                        2007050413

Printed in the United States of America
08 09 10 11 12 RRD 9 8 7 6 5 4 3 2 1

THIS BOOK IS DEDICATED TO THREE WOMEN:

She who prays for a man but sees no change;

she whose son has abandoned the faith; and

she who searches for a Christian mate but finds none.

There is hope.

CONTENTS

INTRODUCTION

Women, Men, and God

Michelangelo captured the relationship between man and his Maker on the ceiling of the Sistine Chapel: A holy God, surrounded by angels, stretches down from heaven to touch the finger of Adam. Meanwhile, the man reclines, nonchalantly extending a single digit toward his Creator.

Why is it so hard to get men to lift a finger for God?

The problem isn't atheism. Nine out of ten men in the United States believe in God.[1] Five out of six men claim to be Christians.[2] Even nonreligious men have a high regard for Jesus Christ and His teachings. But these days it's hard to find a man who puts Jesus first—while it seems like Christian women are as common as boots at a rodeo.

You love Jesus. And you love your men. Naturally, you'd like them to meet. You want your men to know the peace, joy, and contentment that come from an abiding relationship with the Lord.

But these precious men don't seem too interested. Why is it that only preachers, worship leaders, and a few laymen really *get it* when it comes to following Christ? What can you do to help the men you love find the Man you love?

Plenty. Women *can* help men find God. It happens all the time. In fact, research shows that women often play a pivotal role in leading wayward men back to their heavenly Father.[3]

But too often, women's efforts come up short. Women pray daily for the men they love, but nothing happens. They spend years developing their sons' spiritual lives, only to see them forget Jesus during their teens. Their witness to male colleagues falls flat. Single women search in vain for godly men.

Then, a glimmer of hope: Bubba finally gets off the couch and joins you in the pew. You pray like mad, but from the opening hymn it's a total disaster. He feels as out of place as a penguin in the Sahara Desert. His visit reinforces the common male notion: *church just isn't for me.*

This book is not *How to Make Any Man Become a Christian in Three Easy Steps.* Think of it as a Rosetta stone, a key to understanding the mysterious, frustrating, and surprising spiritual lives of the other half of the human race.

Armed with this knowledge, you'll be equipped to fulfill Jesus' call: *Follow Me, and I will make you fishers of men.*

PART ONE

Church Culture vs. Man Culture

It was a hot August day in Houston, Texas. We were rolling down Bellaire Boulevard in our 1964 Chrysler Newport. At the wheel sat my father—raven hair slicked back, a pair of Ray-Ban sunglasses perched on his nose. I sat behind him, my five-year-old legs sweating, sticking to the green vinyl seats.

Suddenly, LOW OIL lit on the dashboard. Dad pulled the Chrysler into a Phillips 66 station to add a quart of Trop-Arctic motor oil. At the double-ding of the alert bell, a man wearing a cap and tie materialized next to the car. The station attendant popped the hood and then called me over to have a look. I was barely tall enough to see over the huge chrome grille.

Wow. This was my first look under the hood of a car. I was amazed at what had been hiding there. I had no idea this crazy tangle of wires, belts, and hoses even existed, much less made the car move.

In the next few chapters, we will be looking *under the hood* of churchgoing. (Yes, I realize this is a guy type of analogy. I'm already training you to think like one of us.) I will shine a bright light on the hidden mechanics of modern Christianity: everything from the Sunday church experience to the structure of our small groups. You may have never considered how these practical, earthly things—in concert with God's Spirit—make the church move. Or how they can unintentionally drive men further from the abundant life.

Women, the LOW OIL light is on. Our car (the church) is still moving forward, but there's trouble brewing. It's time to pop the hood and identify the problem—before all the men are gone.

Where Have All the Good Men Gone?

The sun was nearly set as fifteen women gathered on the deck overlooking Susan's backyard. It was a warm spring evening. The bees buzzed lazily around the bougainvillea as a few crickets began tuning up for their evening of song. The women chatted easily about work, family, and church.

Susan tapped a spoon against her iced tea glass. "Ladies, I'm so glad you've joined us tonight. We are going to devote this evening to supporting one another as we explore what is usually a taboo subject in church today. I mean, have any of you ever talked about this in a group?"

The women shot nervous glances around the circle. A few shook their heads. No one indicated that she had.

Susan continued. "Now, when you received your invitation, I asked you to be ready to answer two questions. I'd like to go around the circle and have everyone very quickly give their names and their answers, OK?"

Heads nodded in agreement.

"I'll start out. My name is Susan, and my number is eight." Susan turned to the woman on her left.

"My name is Juanita, and my number is four."

"My name is Trish, and my number is seven."

"Hello. I'm Theresa, and my number is twenty-three."

The women erupted in gasps, whoops, and laughter. As the noise died down, Theresa clarified, "Hey, I come from a large family!"

The confessions continued. Connie's number was three. Rachel's number was thirteen. Hannah's number was four. Julie's number was ten. And so on.

Once every woman had spoken, Susan added it up. "This small group of women is currently praying for one hundred and thirty-five men. Men we love. Men who need a closer walk with the Lord. That's an average of nine men per person—an average that's much higher, thanks to Theresa!" The women laughed brightly, but inside each carried a dull ache for the spiritual lives of the men they loved.

 **NUMBER, PLEASE**

So let me ask you: what's your number? How many guys are you praying for? How many men in your life need a deeper relationship with Jesus?

Grab a pencil and add it up. Let me help you.

Think about your father. Husband. Ex-husband. Brothers. Uncles. Cousins. Sons. Friends. Boss. Coworkers. Do you have more than ten yet?

I'm not asking whether these men are *spiritual*. I'm not inquiring about their eternal salvation. Nor am I asking if they go to church.

Here's what I want to know: Are these men true disciples of Jesus? Do they enjoy an ongoing, daily walk with God? Are they living a life of love, joy, and peace? Are they connected to a larger community of believers? If not, why not?

Think about your church. Isn't there a significant number of married women who regularly worship without their husbands? Now, how many married men regularly worship without their wives? One or two? Why does it seem that men have a harder time following the Lord than women do?

You're not just imagining it. Christianity is slowly losing its men.

T A LADIES' CLUB? T

Fifty years ago, there would have been no need for a book like this. Men and women attended church in roughly equal numbers.[1] Congregations brimmed with active laymen.

Not anymore.

While the upper echelon of church leadership is mostly male, more than 60 percent of the adults in the typical U.S. worship service are female. The average mainline Protestant congregation is two-thirds female. Many Catholic masses attract a crowd that is 70 percent female.[2] Women compose more than two-thirds of the local church volunteer force and outstrip men in every area of Christian endeavor. They pray more, witness more, and disciple more.[3] Women work while men wimp out.

The gender gap shows up in every age, cultural, and racial group. I wish we could blame Western society for our woes, but the man shortage is a worldwide phenomenon. Christian churches from Minneapolis to Moscow to Melbourne suffer a gender gap. I've received e-mail from pastors overseas whose congregations run 90 percent female.

The men who *do* attend church aren't nearly as involved as the women who outnumber them in the pews. Experts estimate fewer than 10 percent of U.S. churches maintain an ongoing men's ministry.[4] Compare this to the estimated 90 to 95 percent of churches that offer women's and children's ministries.[5]

 Guys and Religion

So why don't we just blame the guys? Aren't men just less religious than women?

Not really. No other religion suffers the huge gender gap Christianity does. In fact, Islam seems to have a bumper crop of men. So did the early church. In Bible days, men were the spiritual giants. Today's spiritual giants wear lipstick and eye shadow.

We have a disconnect here. As I noted in the introduction, 90 percent of U.S. men claim belief in God. Five out of six call themselves Christians. But just two out of six U.S. men claim to have attended church the previous Sunday morning.[6] Some experts believe the true number is fewer than one in six.[7]

That last paragraph may have gotten you thinking, *Those lazy guys! They just need to get their act together and come to church.*

Sure, some guys are lazy. Some are proud. Some are sinful. But in truth, so are some women. Nothing in Scripture suggests that males are born spiritually challenged. Both Adam and Eve fell just as far.

✦ The heart of the matter ✦

I'm going to tell you something that's hard for some women to believe. It may challenge a long-held viewpoint. It may make you mad. But if you cannot accept what I write in the next paragraph, you may as well put this book back on the shelf and ask for a refund.

I'm convinced that in many cases, men's resistance to Christianity is not entirely their fault. This is because, ever so slowly over the centuries, the church has forgotten how to stir the hearts of average guys. Little by little, we've abandoned the male-magnetic methods of Jesus; therefore men have withdrawn.

Now before you ask for that refund, let me clarify something. There are certain men who do quite well in church. Men who grew up religious know the system. Men who are skilled teachers or musicians easily find a place to use their gifts. Men who are sensitive or highly verbal gravitate toward churches. So do studious men who like to read books and debate theology. And unfortunately, predatory men know church is a place they can gain power and control.

But your typical off-the-shelf guy has a hard time *doing church* as it's done today. It's a poor fit for him. So he stays away—or falls asleep.

In days past, societal and family expectations kept men in church. But any social stigma attached to skipping church died years ago. The modern man is completely free to choose whether or not to go to church—and every day more of them choose *not.* The trends are indisputable: churches welcome a lower percentage of men every year.

Women are suffering as a result. In the United States, almost a quarter of married, churchgoing women regularly attend without their husbands.[8] Mothers watch in anguish as their sons turn their backs on Christ during their teens and twenties. Single women comfort themselves with jokes like this one:

SARAH: Have you heard the one about men in the church?
DARCY: No.
SARAH: Men in church are like parking spaces. The good ones are either already taken or they're handicapped.
DARCY: Ha ha. Spiritually speaking, that is.

Sure, there are a few feminists who think men are the problem. They see *too much* male influence in the church and seem to wish the men would just pack up their masculine pronouns and leave. But as I travel the country, that's not what I hear from the women I meet. They want a church with vibrant, spiritually awakened men. Don't you?

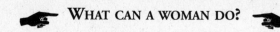

What can a woman do?

If the church routine is not doing a very good job connecting men to God, what can?

Women can. That's why I wrote this book. It is designed to help women just like you:

- discover the root causes of male disinterest in church;
- gain a deeper understanding of men's real spiritual needs;
- learn what women can and can't do to keep their sons engaged at church;
- identify the things about church that drive men crazy—and learn how to change them (or at least understand them);
- develop a way of talking about faith that intrigues men;
- present the gospel in a way men understand;
- identify churches and ministries that speak to both the masculine and feminine heart;
- be challenged to bring more risk and adventure to their personal walk with the Lord; and
- learn how to share with a single man and detect if his faith is real.

In short, this book is a window into the soul of men. And who better to open that window than a man whose faith in Jesus was nearly shipwrecked a few years ago? Here's how it happened to me.

My crisis of faith

Here in Alaska, the sun stays up until midnight in June. I was lying in bed trying to sleep, but the bedroom was too hot and bright. My wife was breathing softly in bed next to me. I pulled back the covers, crept down to the basement, and logged on to the Internet. The session started innocently enough—a little e-mail and a quick check of the latest sports scores. But soon I was visiting Web sites that would shock my wife, my friends, and my church.

I had been a faithful Christian for twenty-four years, a dependable face every Sunday morning. I'd led mission trips, taught Sunday school, and served in every conceivable position in my congregation. I'd recently been elected an elder. But that night my faith was unraveling.

I turned to the Web. I visited two forbidden sites. Two sites intentionally designed to lure men from Christ. They were stimulating. Exciting.

They were Islamic Web sites.

My fellow elders would be horrified. My wife would dissolve in tears. After nearly a quarter of a century of following Jesus, I was tire-kicking a new religion.

I still loved God, but I couldn't bring myself to sit through another church service, Bible study, or committee meeting. I was dying of boredom. My soul craved adventure and challenge; the church offered me study guides. Islam held the promise of strict discipline, high expectations, and male camaraderie. My church was a soft and accepting place that was busy erasing men from hymns, liturgy, and Scripture.

Reading the Bible only made things worse. Its pages were bloodied with bold men taking huge risks for God. Jesus tore through the New Testament like a rogue tornado, challenging, offending, and rebuking with abandon. But my church was a cautious place, and as an elder I was expected to be a careful man who kept the peace. A good Christian was sweet, relational, and above all, *nice*.

I began to wonder if I could be a man and a Christian at the same time. Then it hit me: by my congregation's definition, Jesus Himself would be considered un-Christlike. At best, He'd be considered unfit to lead. At worst, we'd ask Him to leave our church.

Seeking risk, I embarked on some foreign mission trips. I found a modicum of adventure, but I also encountered the same numbing routines in overseas churches—only the services were twice as long.

Back home again, I remember walking through the church atrium in a daze. As I looked around at all the nicely dressed, smiling people drinking coffee and being nice to each other, I thought, *No one would hang on a cross for* this. *There's got to be more.*

Then I began to notice I wasn't the only man who felt this way. I saw the vacant stares, the boredom, the lack of passion. Most of the men were standing in that atrium for three reasons: it was a habit, it was good for the kids, and it kept their wives happy.

Thanks be to God, my faith held. But a holy discontent gripped my heart. I began searching for a book on this subject. None existed. So I began praying. I spent many nights and weekends doing research. Three years later saw the publication of my first book, *Why Men Hate Going to Church.*[9] Men love that book. Almost every day I get grateful e-mail from men who love God but struggle to find their place in the earthly communion of saints.

Men are beginning to understand how they can love God but hate Christian routines. Women, now it's time you understood as well.

YOUR TURN

1. What's your number?

2. Generally speaking, are there more committed laymen or laywomen in your church?

3. Do you think the church shares the blame for men's disinterest in Christianity, or is it mostly the guys' fault?

4. Men and women are obviously different physically and emotionally. Do you think they are different spiritually?

5. The author believes the modern church system is not designed to meet the spiritual needs of most men. Do you agree or disagree? Why?

TAKE ACTION

Ask a man, "What's your opinion of Jesus Christ?" Then ask, "What's your opinion of church services?"

T W O

Man Laws vs. Church Laws

Some time ago, Miller Brewing created an unusual series of commercials titled Man Laws. The ads featured macho men (athletes, coaches, wrestlers, cowboys, and he-man actors, such as Burt Reynolds) sitting around a square table debating the bounds of acceptable male behavior.

Some of the man laws included:

- Men do not iron blue jeans.
- Men do not leave a sporting event early.
- Hugs between men are acceptable, as long as only one arm is used.
- Dating your best friend's ex-girlfriend is allowed after a six-month waiting period.
- When toasting, men do not clink bottles at the top (saliva might be exchanged, which is almost like kissing).

To say these commercials resonated with the public is an understatement. Miller launched a Man Laws Web site, which received more than one hundred thousand suggested additions to the canon.

People liked these ads because they revealed a truth rarely spoken: there exists an unwritten code of masculine behavior that men violate at their peril. Nothing is more important to a man than *being a man*.

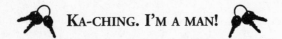

KA-CHING. I'M A MAN!

In *Why Men Hate Going to Church,* I introduced the concept of the *masculinity bank.* As men do things that are considered manly in the eyes of their peers, their bank fills up. This is why young men engage in risky behaviors. It's not about the beer or the women or the guns or the tattoos or the car. They are saying to the world, "Look at me. I'm no longer a boy; I'm a man." Ironic, isn't it? Men often prove their manhood by acting childish.

As men age, they channel their manhood-proving into other pursuits. Some of these are positive. Men get up and go to work when it would be easier to sleep in. Soldiers fight when it would be safer to run. Entrepreneurs build businesses, and fathers raise families. But manhood-proving can also be destructive. Some men become workaholics, abusive, or addicted. Midlife crisis brings the convertible, the gym membership, and sometimes the younger wife. Again, it's not about the car or the girl. It's about *being seen* with the car and the girl. I must admit, when I spot a guy my age with a hot car or a hotter babe, my first thought is, *Man, he's a stud.* As a Christian, I know he's building on sand, but my natural reaction is a twinge of envy.

Women, your eyes may be ready to roll out of their sockets. But you're partly to blame. Even Christian women go for bad boys. Safe guys are boring. They don't get second dates, do they? This is one reason young men would rather die than be perceived as safe or nice. The comic strip *Zits* recently featured teenage Hector's transformation from nerd to dangerous man. Hector got a daring new haircut, dark glasses, and a black sleeveless T-shirt with a skull on it. Girls who never noticed Hector the geek were shamelessly flirting with Hector 2.0.

⚒ CHURCH—A MANLY PLACE? ⚒

Manliness is attractive to both men and women. It's a cornerstone of the male psyche. So reason with me: if a man mentions to his buddies that he goes to church, does this enhance or diminish his standing among his peers? In other words, does a man's status as a practicing Christian add to his masculinity bank or deplete it?

If you are honest, the answer is obvious. Many men perceive churchgoing as unmanly. It's the polar opposite of the risky, dangerous image they try to project. So they avoid it. They don't go to church for the same reason they don't carry a purse—it's not something guys do.

Some men can safely go to church because it's obvious they're not very religious. For example, a Mafia don may attend mass. But is he a true follower of Jesus? *Fugeddaboudit.*

One Saturday, I polled men outside a sportsmen's show in Anchorage, Alaska. Ninety-five guys responded to this query: "I'm going to read a list of twelve places where people gather. Please tell me whether these places have a more feminine feel or a more masculine feel."

Here's what the guys said:

	Masculine	Feminine	Undecided
Football Stadium	83	1	11
Baby Shower	0	95	0
Flower Shop	4	74	17
Gun Show	85	1	9
Elementary School	1	54	40
Church Service	*11*	*30*	*54*
Hospital	14	27	54
Bar	59	2	34
Fishing Boat	76	0	19
Shopping Mall	1	67	27
Sunday School	*3*	*50*	*42*
Office Building	26	19	50

As you can see, church services and Sunday school were perceived as feminine more often than masculine. Only eleven men perceived church as masculine, and just three perceived Sunday school as manly. It's not a shutout like baby showers (which all ninety-five men saw as girly). But it's clear that lots of men pick up the scent of a woman in our houses of worship.[1]

Why does this matter? Because a man won't do something he believes is feminine. It costs too many coins from his masculinity bank. This is why men don't hang out at baby showers, flower shops, craft bazaars, or froufrou boutiques. *What will the guys think?*

⌐ But there's a man in the pulpit! ¬

You may be confused. Many women have assumed that church is a men's club, male dominated and patriarchal. It's easy to see why one might come to this conclusion. Ninety-five percent of the senior pastors in America are men.[2] Every Catholic priest is a man. Some church boards are composed entirely of men. Because males dominate the top floor of church leadership, at first glance the church seems like a bastion of masculine power.

Think of the local church as a ship. The captain is likely to be male, but his officers and crew will be primarily female. A study from Barna research found that women were 56 percent more likely than men to have held a leadership position in church and 33 percent more likely to volunteer.[3]

The composition of the crew has a profound effect on the captain. If he wants the ship to run smoothly, he must be able to please and motivate women. Clergymen learn early in their careers: *if Mama ain't happy, ain't nobody happy.* Should the skipper run afoul of certain powerful women, he'll have a mutiny on his hands. The ministry engines will sputter and die. So pastors work overtime to make women feel loved and needed. Studies by Gallup and Barna find men trailing far behind women in Christian faith practice, so few pastors invest in men.[4] What's the point?

Our pastors may be from Mars, but Christian values come from Venus. Whenever people describe the character of Jesus, you hear words such as *loving, tender, gentle,* and *compassionate.* This is how men and women, Christians and non-Christians alike, describe our Lord. Rarely does anyone call Him *frightening, commanding, stern,* or *zealous,* even though eyewitnesses chose these very words to capture His personality.

So yes, there's a man in the pulpit. But he's leading a church that's primarily female, whose lay leaders are mostly women, and whose values come from Venus.

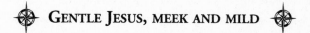

GENTLE JESUS, MEEK AND MILD

This is not a new problem. The church has a long history of marginalizing men and masculinity. If you want a more detailed explanation, read my first book, *Why Men Hate Going to Church.* I offer the briefest of overviews here, so you can learn to recognize this drift in your own congregation. Here are six reasons the masculine spirit consistently disappears from our churches:

1. Jesus' Most Famous Teachings Are His Softest Ones.

Christ encountered a Jewish religious tradition that was harshly masculine, controlling, and legalistic. So His most famous teachings were those that stood in contrast:

- "Blessed are the meek" (Matt. 5:5).
- "Judge not, that you be not judged" (Matt. 7:1).
- "If someone strikes you on the right cheek, turn to him the

other also" (Matt. 5:39 NIV).

- "Do to others what you would have them do to you" (Matt. 7:12 NIV).
- "Love your enemies" (Matt. 5:44).
- "Come to Me . . . and I will give you rest" (Matt. 11:28).

Since these teachings of Jesus get the most press, Christianity's public image equates to a rather soft, weak religion. As Christians, we embrace weakness so God's strength can shine through (2 Cor. 12:10). But an obsessive focus on weakness can freeze a church in its tracks, crowding out Christ's call to faith, boldness, and action.

2. The Doctrine of Grace Is Harder for Men to Swallow.

Christianity stands alone among great religions in that salvation is a free gift that cannot be earned. This is the good news of the gospel. But this is not such good news for performance-oriented males. God created Adam to work. Men want to earn by the sweat of their brows and are deeply skeptical of anything that's offered free. And men hate to accept help—even from God.

It's hard for men to *be saved*. Throughout the literature of hundreds of cultures, men are almost always the saviors, while women are the ones being saved. Today's Hollywood blockbusters still follow this ancient formula—Spider-Man rescues Mary Jane, not the other way around. It goes against the cultural grain for a man to assume the role of damsel in distress.

I'm not trashing the doctrine of grace. Without grace, Christianity crumbles. I'm simply pointing out that a man will feel the need to earn his salvation more often than a woman will. That's one reason that here in the United States, alternative religions that base salvation on good works are more popular with men than women.[5]

3. As a Congregation Matures, Masculine Values Are Pushed Aside.

Young churches are magnets to men, because they are built on values they find attractive. Church plants are externally focused, goal oriented, and stubbornly orthodox in belief. Their survival depends on strategic planning and bold initiatives. Eventually they need a building. Men dig this stuff, and they have a lot to offer in these arenas.

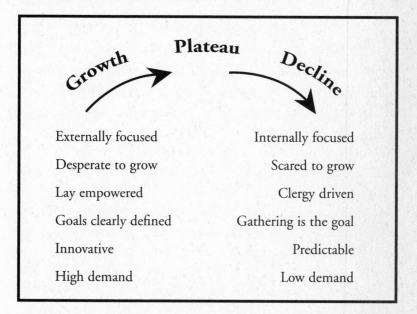

Growth	Plateau	Decline
Externally focused		Internally focused
Desperate to grow		Scared to grow
Lay empowered		Clergy driven
Goals clearly defined		Gathering is the goal
Innovative		Predictable
High demand		Low demand

But once a church reaches a certain size, it stabilizes. The building gets finished, cash flow firms up, and a core membership is in place. So the congregation makes a subtle shift from offense to defense. The focus changes from fishing for men to creating a comfortable aquarium for the saints.

Men get bored playing defense. The inevitable infighting, backbiting, and hypocrisy send them for the lifeboats. Once the men are overboard, the young people follow. Women stay aboard because the church is their relational network, but without the wind of the Spirit in their sails, they drift.

The same process affects denominations. They are born ortho-dox, high demand, and externally focused. They die lenient, low demand, and focused on internal turf wars.

4. The Church Has a History of Marginalizing Laymen.

In the years after Pentecost, enthusiastic laymen spearheaded the widespread growth of the church. But since the conversion of the Roman emperor Constantine in AD 312, the church has tended to institutionalize power, stripping laymen of their roles and assigning these to professional clergy. Then a reformation, restoration, or revival breaks out and laymen get involved again. The church grows. But over time, the church reinstitutionalizes, leaving laymen with little influence. They fall away.

5. The Victorian Era Brought an Explosion of Femininity to the Church.

During the nineteenth century, the Industrial Revolution changed the composition of the western church. Large numbers of men left their homes to work in mines, mills, and factories. Who remained to fill the pews? Women, children, and elderly men. The able-bodied male all but disappeared from Sunday worship.

In their absence, Victorian women reinvented ministry accord-ing to their talents. Their innovations included Sunday school, church nursery, youth group, soup kitchens, women's choirs, ladies' social circles, and temperance unions, to name a few. Men, on the other hand, found their fellowship in secular groups such as the Shriners, Freemasons, Elks, Moose, and VFW. They formed service clubs such as Rotary, Lions, and Kiwanis.

With Victorian worship services running 65 to 75 percent female, feminine expression became the norm in the church. Hymns became less militaristic and more romantic. Sermons came to focus on family and relationships. Corporate worship began to embrace sentimentality and personal expression. Prayer-and-share, personal testimonies, and emotional revivalism swept the church. The Pentecostal movement (which began in 1906) amplified these trends.

6. Western Thought Assigned Religion to the Realm of Feelings.

Before the Industrial Revolution, families worked together on farms or in shops. Then everything changed. Work became specialized by gender. Men were employed outside the home, while women labored in the domestic sphere.

This development coincided with the Enlightenment, the Age of Reason, and the ascension of science as the font of truth. By the end of the nineteenth century, a completely new worldview engulfed the West, which Nancy Pearcey calls the "public/private split."[6]

	Led by	Key traits	Arenas	Focus
PUBLIC REALM	Men High-Achieving Women	Verifiable Competitive Strenuous Hierarchical Masculine Stoic	Military Government Science Business Higher Education Sports	Externals Objects Facts
PRIVATE REALM	Women Underachieving Men	Taken on Faith Cooperative Comforting Egalitarian Feminine Emotional	Relationships Family & Children Religion Personal Growth Home Elementary Education	Internals Intangibles Intuition

This worldview essentially ushered God out of the public square. The more religion came to be seen as a private matter, the less acceptable it became for a man to have any interest in it. (Note that this worldview has not yet taken hold in the East, so men on the other side of the globe remain fervent, public participants in organized religion.)

⚓ "Religion is her responsibility" ⚓

As you can see, there are many reasons men think, *Church is for chicks.* And there are constant societal and institutional pressures that squeeze men and their values out of congregational life.

Meet Claude. Raised in church, he left it during his teens. Five years ago he married Janet, and they have a daughter who is in the midst of the terrible twos. He is watching his little angel start to lie, steal, and throw tantrums. Suddenly the doctrine of original sin makes sense to Claude. He's willing to go back to church since his daughter needs moral instruction—and fast! But Claude would no sooner choose a church than choose drapes. Religion belongs in his wife's basket of responsibilities, along with family, relationships, childcare, and education. Claude sees Janet as better qualified to make decisions in spiritual matters.

Does this scenario sound familiar? We have millions of Claudes (or clods) who have handed the reins of religious responsibility to their wives. It's not that they're lazy. They simply think that religion is not a man's role. These men feel deep in their hearts that the Christian faith is for women, children, and professional clergymen.

MEN DON'T DO PINK

Have you ever returned a rental car to the airport? If so, you've probably driven over those spiked barriers that keep cars from being stolen. It's perfectly safe to cross the barrier in one direction. But cross it the wrong way, and you'll end up with four flat tires.

So it is with gender roles in our society: women cross easily into male roles, but men who cross into female roles risk an identity blowout. For example, we have tomboys, but no *tomgirls*. Almost half the student athletes at my daughter's high school are now girls, but boys make up less than 3 percent of her dance troupe. Women are breaking glass ceilings in the workplace, but men don't even try for so-called women's jobs—even those that pay well. For example, almost half of the doctors in the United States are women, but only 6 percent of America's nurses are men.[7]

Bottom line: women do masculine, but men don't do feminine. So if a man perceives church or Sunday school as a feminine thing, he will quickly excuse himself. It costs him too many coins. Men don't do pink.

So do men think church is pink? Just ask Harley the heathen.

Harley shows up in church. Within moments of stepping into the building, Harley is forced to bend or break multiple man laws. He enters a facility adorned with quilts, flowers, and lace. Harley looks around the sanctuary and sees many more women than men. The bulletin offers him a chance to volunteer in the nursery, cook for a potluck dinner, join a scrapbooking group, or attend a ladies' Bible study.

We ask Harley to sing love songs to another man: "Jesus, Lover of My Soul"; "You are Beautiful, My Sweet, Sweet Song"; and "He Touched Me." We speak a foreign language (Christianese) and expect him to participate in rituals without explaining them (so he feels inadequate). Several women stand up and share prayer requests for people he does not know. Men value their personal space, but the church seems intent on violating it: *Turn to your neighbor and give him a great, big hug. Let's all hold hands. Sit in a circle and share what's on your heart.*

Harley is supposed to sit still for a lecture (sermon) that can run anywhere from twenty minutes to two hours. He's supposed to give money with no idea what it's going toward. Once the service is over, the real agony comes: chatting with people he doesn't know.

By the time he escapes to the parking lot, Harley's masculinity bank is punctured and leaking badly. He is so far out of his comfort zone he'd need a GPS to find it again.

The early church did away with mandatory circumcision, but today's church unwittingly emasculates its men. It's almost as if we're saying, "Welcome to church. You won't be needing those; check them at the door."

⤙ Don't be swept downstream ⤚

Must we expunge every trace of femininity from our churches? Certainly not. The goal is balance. But not 50–50 balance. Right now, most Christian organizations are tilted slightly toward the feminine. A church that wants to grow will tip the balance slightly toward the masculine. Remember, both men and women are drawn to the things of men. If we want to engage all persons, our churches should speak with a masculine accent. In chapter 8, you'll learn how churches are doing this without driving women away.

Have you ever sat in a fishing boat on a swiftly moving river? If you want to stay in place, you have to troll—that is, run your engine at a low speed that keeps you from being swept downstream. The moment you stop fighting the current, you begin to drift.

In this chapter, we identified the many currents that push our churches toward feminine values, expression, and reputation. If we want to avoid being swept downstream, we need to keep pushing toward the masculine. Congregations that stop fighting for men and boys drift slowly toward comfort, safety, and irrelevance. They eventually plunge over the falls to their deaths.

YOUR TURN

1. Many women assume the church is male dominated. What do you think?

2. Why do you think declining churches tend to lose their men first?

3. In what ways do you detect a feminine tilt in your church?

4. Should we tip the balance toward the masculine in our ministries? Why or why not?

5. Let's say current trends continue, and by the year 2100 the worldwide church is more than 75 percent female. Most of our ministers will be female. What do you think our congregational life will be like?

TAKE ACTION

Count the adults in your worship service next Sunday. Calculate the gender ratio. Share your findings with the leaders of your congregation.

THREE

The House of Horrors

The cricket choir was in full song as fifteen women continued sharing their stories. Susan lit a half dozen tiki torches to provide light and to keep a few early-season mosquitoes at bay.

Trish was next to share. "Easter was a couple of weeks ago, so my husband made his annual trip to church," she said. "You could tell he was nervous. He had this look in his eyes . . ."

"Like a deer in the headlights?" asked Juanita.

"No, it's like he didn't want me to know he was afraid. So he acted all nonchalant. But you could tell he was uncomfortable the whole time. During the singing, he gripped the pew so tightly his knuckles turned white." She paused. "During the sermon, I sat there next to him, praying the gospel would get through. But I could tell it wasn't. When we got out into the parking lot, I could sense his relief."

The other women nodded as if to say, *We've been there too, sister.* Then Trish added, "The only other time I've seen my husband like this is when I took him for a colonoscopy."

Trish hadn't meant to be funny, but several women giggled at the comparison. You have got to wonder which experience men find more painful: sitting on a camera or sitting through a church service.

THE TOP TEN THINGS MEN FEAR MOST ABOUT CHURCH

Though they probably wouldn't admit it, many men are afraid to go to church. That's right: afraid. The house of God has become a house of horrors. To help you understand why, I've prepared a list for you of the top ten things men fear most about the Christian life. I want you to understand these fears so you can pray specifically against them—and offer your man the proper encouragement as he overcomes his fears.

Before I begin, let me issue the following disclaimers:

- Fear is no excuse for a man to ignore the call of God on his life.
- By listing these fears, I'm not attempting to pardon men or to elicit sympathy on your part.
- The following fears do not affect every man. Your guy may experience only one or two of these fears, or none at all.
- Men experience these fears in varying degrees.
- A salvation experience or religious awakening will often help a man overcome his fears. In other words, he'll be so drawn to God that these fears fade into the background. But they can surface later, causing men to become disenchanted with church and drop the faith entirely.
- Many of these fears subside as men get older. The need to be macho, hip, and stylish fades as a man ages. (This is one reason older men are more religious than younger men.)
- If you ask a man if he's afraid of these things, he'll probably say no. Men are usually unaware of what they fear or are unwilling to admit they're afraid.

We've already exposed one of men's biggest fears in chapter 2: *church forces a man to violate multiple man laws.* Now we examine ten other fears to help you appreciate the panic that grips his heart when you ask, "Would you like to go to church with me?"

10. "I'll Hate Church, Like When I Was a Kid."

Men often have a harder time forgetting a traumatic experience than women do. This is because of a difference in brain structure.[1] So if men were traumatized in church as children, they're more likely than women to retain those fears as adults.

Since the majority of U.S. men were raised in church (at least for a time), they bear some childhood memories of it. And if those memories are bad, they may feel distressed every time they enter a house of worship. The sight of stained glass or the smell of musty hymnals can summon vivid, painful memories years later.

It doesn't take horrific abuse to create negative childhood memories. Some boys were just bored out of their minds—and they're loath to repeat the experience as adults. As a little boy, I remember sitting through lengthy church services wearing a stiff-collared shirt and choking necktie, my feet squeezed into uncomfortable patent leather shoes. At the ripe old age of seven, I made myself a promise: *once I'm grown up, I'm never going to do this again.* Fortunately God found me as a teen, but most men who utter this vow keep it the rest of their lives.

One reason contemporary churches seem to do a better job reaching men is their rejection of old-time religion. Their modern style doesn't stir up painful memories of childhood. Of course, some men had a wonderfully positive church upbringing, and these are the fellows you are most likely to find in the pews of traditional churches.

9. "I'll Lose Control."

A man's greatest fear is *powerlessness,* whereas a woman most fears *loneliness.* A man's worst nightmare is to become completely disabled, utterly dependent on others. A woman's worst fear is to be abandoned, left alone, and unloved.

When Sam and Sally go to church, they hear a message like this: *you need to give control of your life to God and enter into a personal relationship with the One who will never leave you or forsake you.* For Sam to embrace this message, he would have to face his deepest fear—loss of control. But for Sally, the gospel means she'll never have to face her fear—she'll never be unloved. Who's getting the more attractive offer?

There are many other controls a man must give up when going to church. For instance, he loses control of his time. If a church service is long, boring, irrelevant, or weird, he's stuck. Out of politeness, people rarely just get up and leave. So Sam feels trapped. *I gave up my weekend for this?* he thinks.

Men fear being singled out for attention at church. Most guys would rather come and go anonymously, but in many churches we ask visitors to stand and be recognized. Men usually hate this attention.

To my Pentecostal readers, I must tell you that many men fear the emotionally charged atmosphere common in Spirit-filled worship. One man I interviewed said he felt like he was trapped in a freak show when people around him began speaking in tongues, weeping and wailing loudly, and passing out at the altar.

Why do men look askance at these things? Consider how males are raised in our society. From the crib they're taught that big boys don't cry; strong men keep their emotions in check. (We all know how harmful this ethos is to men's mental health; nevertheless, it is drilled into our sons' hearts from an early age.)

So when Sam and Sally walk into a Spirit-filled church, emotions run high. Everyone is supposed to drop their guard and get jiggy with Jesus. This is much harder for Sam than for Sally because he's breaking an ingrained social taboo. Sally can lose control, because women face no sanction for a public display of emotion.

8. "I'll Get Stuck with Some Weirdo."

According to an article in *Christianity Today*, who is America's most famous evangelical? It's not a televangelist, politico, or megachurch pastor. It's Ned Flanders, the Bible-quoting, teetotaling neighbor on the animated TV series *The Simpsons*.[2] Ned's a stereotypical Jesus nut who's cheery, straightlaced, and . . . nerdy. Flanders is the nicest guy you could ever meet, and if you think he's weird, that's just *okely-dokely* with him.

There's a certain peculiarity that comes from following closely after God (think John the Baptist), but some Christians have taken weird to a new level (think diamond-encrusted televangelist). We've all known Christians who have gotten excited about the Lord and gone completely off the end of the pier.

Some men fear if they were to become religious, they might end up like Flanders. Or they'll find themselves in some secret assembly of wide-eyed religious fanatics. ("Excuse me, could you pass the Kool-Aid, please?")

Men also fear that a life of faith spells the end of fun. Men don't understand that following God can be a blast, because it doesn't look like a blast. Giving up your weekends to sing songs and listen to sermons doesn't sound appealing to your average guy. Christians also have a reputation as straightlaced prudes who "don't drink, don't smoke, don't dance, don't play cards, don't go to movies, and don't associate with those who do." Most men would rather attend a dull party than a great Bible study.

7. "I Don't Trust the Other Men."

I remember the good old days when preachers used to have affairs with women.

Today's headlines shriek: PASTOR ACCUSED OF INAPPROPRIATELY TOUCHING MEN. MINISTER DEFROCKED FOR GAY RELATIONSHIP. PRIEST ACCUSED OF MOLESTING BOYS. Then there are headlines like these: CHURCH DEBATES GAY MARRIAGE. DENOMINATION ELEVATES GAY BISHOP. The media has worked overtime associating the words *church* and *gay*, to the point that men are starting to think we're chock-full of closeted Liberaces.

They're not far from the truth. Homosexuality is widespread in many churches today. Former priest Richard Sipe estimates that in the United States, at least half of Catholic priests and a third of the bishops are gay.[3] If you're a black man looking for a homosexual hookup, just go to church. So says J. L. King, a bisexual who claims to have found multiple male sex partners in African American congregations. King said, "There are gospel [music] conventions throughout the nation for churches. These events allow men to meet and to have sex while away from their hometowns. Many midnight concerts turn into affairs where brothers are cruising each other. I've been there, seen it, and done it."[4] Michael Stevens, an African American pastor from North Carolina, says that in many congregations it's a not-so-quiet secret among parishioners that their minister is involved in secret homosexual relationships—even as he thunders against the practice from the pulpit.[5]

These gay undercurrents can cause a man to keep the church at arm's length. The fear of an unwanted advance makes guys think twice before joining a men's small group or meeting with a guy from the church for coffee. It suppresses attendance at the annual men's retreat. Some men are afraid to send their sons to church camps or allow the boy to be mentored by another man. *What if he's a pervert?*

6. "If I Become a Christian, I'll Become Soft."

Women are tough. I didn't realize how tough until I watched my daughter coming through the birth canal. Hardy as women are, though, they don't usually brag about it. Sure, we have female triathletes who compare their times and BMIs, but most women don't measure themselves by how rugged they are.

Men do. And many fear that if they turn to Christ, they will soften, lose their killer instinct, and fall behind their competitors, becoming weak. Jesse Ventura, a former governor, pro wrestler, and Navy SEAL spoke for millions of men when he said, "Organized religion is a sham and a crutch for weak-minded people who need strength in numbers."[6] The religion he was referring to was ours.

Why do men think Christians are wimps? Because that's what church culture is trying to produce. Paul Coughlin writes of Christian men, "The church tells them they should rarely if ever exert their will, that possessing passion, boldness and intensity is wrong and 'worldly.' Those qualities belong to 'aggressive' and 'proud' men. (ironically, including Jesus) Many have told me that it's far more Christian to live limply, deny your heart's desires, and keep your life in neutral because somehow, brother, this glorifies God."[7]

5. "I'm Single—and Church Is Tough."

Single guys ages eighteen to thirty-five are the demographic least likely to attend church—and we don't make it easy on them. I have a number of single, churchgoing buddies who describe the subtle pressure they feel to settle down and get married. One friend of mine (a single man in his thirties) says the matrons of the congregation are constantly asking if he's got a girlfriend. He's even had one offer to be his matchmaker. And since there are so few eligible bachelors in his church, going to a singles' meeting feels like "walking into a room full of bees with honey smeared on your face."

Becoming a Christian also means that one must bring his sexual life into line with scriptural standards. Thanks to their higher levels of testosterone, young men generally have a higher sex drive than young women. They fear that if they were to become Christ-followers, they would not be able to contain the fire that burns within.

Chastity carries a higher social price for men, because among guys, promiscuity has long been considered manly. Meanwhile, women who sleep around have been considered cheap. Abstinence erodes a man's status among his peers, while it enhances a woman's standing among hers. I'm not saying this is right; it's just the way society has traditionally viewed sexuality.

Believe it or not, churchgoing can actually inflame lust in a man's heart. It's a weekly appointment with throngs of women who look their best. Contemporary churches attract lots of young women—many of whom dress provocatively, to say the least. The exposed cleavage and tight-fitting garments that made spring break famous are now appearing at a worship service near you. Young women, I ask you to help the men by practicing modesty—especially at church. You can look nice without dressing like a dancer on MTV.

I talked to one man who had to change churches because of this issue. A particularly well-built young woman would regularly go forward to wave a flag during worship. She usually wore an embarrassingly tight tank top and jiggled sensually during the praise music. "I know this woman just wanted to praise her Savior, but her dancing was very suggestive," he said. "All she lacked was a brass pole." I suggested he mortify his flesh by joining a mainline congregation. Lust is no problem in a church where the average woman is pushing sixty.

4. "Church Is Full of Hypocrites."

What's the number one excuse you'll hear from men who avoid church? *There are too many hypocrites.* Men expect perfection from the church, and they feel entitled to point out its shortcomings. Why is hypocrisy such a problem for men but not for women?

Perhaps the answer lies on the cover of *Family Circle*. At least four times a year, this women's magazine features a cover shot of some scrumptious-looking dessert oozing with chocolate, cream, and nuts. And printed just above this eight-hundred-calorie delicacy is a headline that says: LOSE 10 LBS. IN 3 WEEKS. Ladies, that's hypocrisy. There is an obvious contradiction between the headline and the photo. But women don't see hypocrisy; they see hope. So they keep buying *Family Circle* every month.

Pastor Mark Gungor believes men avoid church because they know if they hear the Word, they would have to become doers of the Word (James 1:22–25).[8] They know their lives don't measure up to God's standards, so they skip church out of a sense of integrity. They wouldn't want to become hypocrites themselves.

3. "All They Want Is My Money."

In our society, men are supposed to earn a good living and accumulate possessions. And nothing makes a bigger statement than the car they drive.

> Jeff Quackenbush's daily commute was making him feel like a "girly man." For months, the burly Orlando, Florida, businessman had been forced to drive his wife's minivan because he couldn't afford a new set of wheels. But then came the zero-percent-financing bonanza General Motors rolled out after 9/11 to lure car buyers back into its deserted showrooms. Quackenbush raced down to his local Chevrolet dealer and snapped up a hulking $40,000 black pickup truck . . . He said, "I feel like a man again. Thank you, GM."[9]

Having the right stuff is important to men. It's one way they prove their manhood. A big, bad truck, a trophy home, a nice boat. Like it or not, men size each other up by what they own. (Churchgoing guys are no exception, believe me.)

This need underlies men's most common complaint about church: "All they want is my money." The church wants it both ways: a man is supposed to drop 10 percent in the plate, but he gets in trouble for working too many hours. Giving not only affects his bank balance but it also crimps his ability to prove himself through the accumulation of possessions.

Once a man starts giving, he discovers God gives back. Still, this lesson can be harder for a man to learn because society expects him to be flush.

2. "I'm Jealous."

When Sally falls in love with Jesus, Sam is naturally jealous. If she had fallen for the gardener, at least Sam could march into the yard and give the interloper a black eye. But how is a man supposed to compete with someone he can't even see?

Some women fall hard for Jesus; others for the church—or the pastor. Sabrina Black recalls a time when she returned from church to her husband's withering stare. "If I want anything done around here, all I need to do is call the church and let your pastor tell you, because you do what the pastor says to do," he said. "When the pastor says he needs somebody, you come running. When the pastor says there is a committee or a project, you show up. If I ask you to do something, you are too busy."[10]

Sons also notice when Mom is gone all the time, feeding her savior complex. Boys think, *Church is something that takes Mother away.* Sons can become just as resentful as husbands, but they may not feel entitled to speak up.

How do you balance your love for Christ and His church with love for the men in your household? We will discuss this important issue at length in chapter 15.

1. "I'm Being Held to an Impossible Standard."

Thanks to women's magazines, TV shows, and Dr. Phil, married men are held to a pretty high standard these days. But Christian husbands are supposed to be perfect, right? Dr. Kevin Leman, author of *Sheet Music (Uncovering the Secrets of Sexual Intimacy in Marriage)* says, "Not only are [Christian] men supposed to attend morning Bible studies, but they're also supposed to get home in time for dinner, spend time alone with each child, date their wives once a week, and earn enough money so that their wives can stay home with their young children. This is a heavy load, and some Christian men start to resent it."[11]

While Christian women's books focus on a multiplicity of goals, almost every religious book for men is focused on a single target: making better husbands and fathers. Men's ministry meetings pound the same drum. *Be a better husband and father. Keep your promises. If your wife isn't happy, you're to blame.* Family harmony received scant attention from Jesus. How did it become the primary focus of men's ministry? After a while a man begins to wonder, *Is the church in league with my wife?*

We don't hound Christian women to be better mothers and wives. In church, the unspoken assumption is that men are broken and in need of repair. Nancy Wray Gegoire wrote, "I've often noticed that sermons on Mother's Day tend to gush over moms, while on Father's Day they tell dads to shape up."[12] No wonder men skulk away like dogs that have been kicked one time too many.

ꝑ

DESPITE THESE AND other fears, millions of men come to church every weekend. They bravely defy the man laws, quash their fears, and make their way to God's house. But waiting for them behind those stained-glass windows lay the biggest horror of all. We'll identify the sum of all male fears in our next chapter.

YOUR TURN

1. Are men really afraid of church? If so, why?

2. Do you think of Christian men as softer than other men? Why do men think this?

3. Look back over the top ten list. As you think about one of the men you're praying for, which fear affects him most?

- I'll hate church, like when I was a kid.
- I'll lose control.
- I'll get stuck with some weirdo.
- I don't trust the other men.
- If I become a Christian, I'll become soft.
- I'm single—and church is tough.
- Church is full of hypocrites.
- All they want is my money.
- I'm jealous.
- I'm being held to an impossible standard.

4. Some men become jealous of Jesus because they feel women love Him more. But aren't women supposed to love God first? Where is the balance point?

5. Be honest: when you hear of a Christian family in crisis, do you assume the man is to blame? Why?

TAKE ACTION

Show a man the top ten list in question 3. Ask him if he can relate to any of these fears.

FOUR

The Stars vs. the Scrubs

Peg spoke next. "I'm embarrassed even bringing this up. I know many of you would give your right arm to see your men in church. Well, my guy goes to church pretty consistently, but that's it. He has no discernible Christian life beyond worship services." A couple of women leaned forward in their chairs and nodded in agreement.

Peg continued. "He says he believes in God, but I just don't sense the Holy Spirit working in his life. And he's not the only man in our church like this. They tried to get a men's retreat together last month, but they had to cancel it when only four guys signed up."

Peg is right. Not only is it hard to get guys in the door, but once they're inside it's nearly impossible to get them to participate. An illustration from the game of basketball may help you understand why.

MEET THE SCRUBS

A men's NBA team has fifteen players. But only eight or nine play during a typical game. These players are known as the *stars*. The rest of the players are nicknamed *scrubs*. The scrubs are also known as benchwarmers, because that is what they do night after night. Their only hope of seeing action is if one of the stars is forced to leave the game due to injury, cold shooting, or foul trouble.

What is the difference between a star and a scrub? Natural ability. The stars are the most talented players, while the scrubs are somewhat less talented. Scrubs are decent players, but they lack the full complement of skills the stars bring to the game.

It's tough being a scrub. They work just as hard, exercise just as much, and suit up for every game, but they rarely get to play because somebody else is a little bit better than they are. They get discouraged.

Where am I going with this? Hold on.

A MAN'S GREATEST FEAR

In the previous chapter, I promised to reveal a man's greatest fear. Here you go: *a man's greatest fear is to be found incompetent.* Men are absolutely horrified when they mess up or are outshone by someone else.

Therefore, a man will gravitate toward things he is good at, while avoiding anything that calls his skills into question. This is why men refuse to ask for directions. And why many men avoid going to church.

When it comes to churchgoing, most women are potential stars, while most men are potential scrubs. Why? Natural ability. The average woman possesses the skills that allow her to participate fully in the game. But the average man lacks the churchgoing skills that come so naturally to women.

I'm not talking about spiritual gifts; I'm referring to the mundane, practical abilities that allow a person to function at a high level in a gathering of Christians.

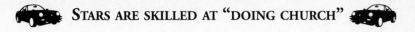

STARS ARE SKILLED AT "DOING CHURCH"

The natural abilities that help a person become a star in church can be summed up in three words: *verbal*, *studious*, and *sensitive*.

A churchgoer must be *verbal*:

- Churchgoers must enjoy listening to spoken lessons and sermons.
- They should be practiced at the art of conversation and small talk.
- Top-tier stars possess the verbal fluency to preach, teach, pray aloud, and comment in small groups.

A churchgoer must be *studious*:

- Churchgoers must be good readers and are expected to love studying.
- Top performers can find texts in books, analyze these texts, and form conclusions.
- The ability to lecture and teach is a huge plus.

A churchgoer must be *sensitive*:

- Churchgoers must enjoy socializing.
- They must be emotionally perceptive and tenderhearted.
- Their primary focus should be relationships, family, and children.
- Churchgoers should be introspective and thoughtful.
- They must love music and singing.

Any person—male or female—who possesses these skills is a potential Sunday morning star. Multiple studies, surveys, and polls have shown that women are more likely than men to fit the profile. Here's how it breaks down.

A Star Has Verbal Skills

Anne and Bill Moir wrote, "This basic difference between men and women is fundamental and is confirmed by an extraordinarily wide body of research: women are generally more verbal, men are more spatial. She is good with words, he is good with things."[1] Boys are more likely to graduate high school lacking basic reading and writing skills. They're more likely to be dyslexic and less likely to read for pleasure.[2] These differences persist into adulthood.

Now think about church. From the moment you walk in the doors, it's a Niagara Falls of verbal stimuli: sermons, Bible readings, study guides, spoken lessons, responsive readings, and song lyrics, not to mention spoken prayers and after-service conversation. It's obvious that a person with abundant verbal fluency will derive the most joy from church.

A Star Is Studious

Although many of our top scholars are men, more women gravitate toward education. About three-quarters of girls graduate from high school, while only about two-thirds of boys do. Women attend college at higher rates than men, where they compose 56 percent of the undergraduate student population and 59 percent of graduate students.[3]

Much of the modern Christian life is built on an academic model: we offer Sunday *school,* Bible *study,* vacation Bible *school,* and Christian *education.* About half the square footage in our churches is devoted to classroom space. The centerpiece of Protestant worship is the sermon, which is a lecture by another name. Church is a teaching institution you never graduate from.

A Star Is Sensitive

You don't need a study to confirm that women are often more sensitive than men. The average female is more concerned with relationships, more child oriented, and more emotionally perceptive than the typical male. Concerning music: doesn't it seem like girls are more likely than boys to receive formal music training as children? I recently attended my daughter's piano recital, where I heard twenty-six girls and five boys perform. Women's early exposure to music helps them appreciate our second most popular church pastime: singing.

Of course, these are all generalities. Certain men can outtalk, outstudy, and outempathize any woman. Some men are virtuoso musicians, gifted teachers, or obsessive bookworms. But considering both genders as a whole, the gifts and experiences that make one an ideal churchgoer are more commonly found among the fairer sex.

⚒ STARS FIT THE VOLUNTEER PROFILE ⚒

It's not just her natural abilities that allow the female to soar above the male in church. Most volunteer opportunities involve roles that have historically belonged to women. The average U.S. congregation of eighty-four members needs volunteers in seven main areas:

- Childcare
- Teaching
- Music
- Cooking
- Gatherings (weddings, funerals, showers.)
- Committees
- Ushering

Given this list of opportunities, where do most men end up? "Here's your bulletin, ma'am. Can I help you find a seat?"

Are there brothers willing to change diapers in the nursery, teach Sunday school, and put on a choir robe? Of course there are, and

God bless them. But these have been women's roles for centuries, and many men feel ill-qualified or even embarrassed in them.

Ministries such as these change the core competencies of a Christian. The star disciple is no longer the most verbal, studious, and sensitive. A man who can wield a saw feels valued and needed. He's got a skill that he can use for God's kingdom—something he can do better than his wife. It's his turn to shine.

For stars, churchgoing comes easy

There's a reason our pews are filled with women. There are more females in the population whose skills and experiences match the culture of the church. In short, most women are potential stars.

But guys? Most are potential scrubs. They know it too. They lack the natural abilities to excel in church; therefore they focus their time and energy in venues where they can be stars. The workplace. The golf course. The fishing boat. These are oases of male competence.

Joey is a furnace repairman. He's a star at installing and maintaining heating and cooling systems. He's good with his hands and can repair almost anything. He's also a skilled hunter and fisherman.

But get him into a church, and suddenly he's a scrub. He lacks the skills one needs to be a good churchgoer. His abilities (fixing things, troubleshooting, and project management) are almost useless in church. He's not very good at study, chit-chat, or childcare. Joey believes in God, but church leaves him bored and frustrated.

What's worse, the man who runs the church is a star. The worship leader is a star. The guy who teaches adult Sunday school is a star. That fellow on the front row who's raising his hands and crying is a star.

As these men shine, Joey feels even more like a scrub.

It gets worse. Stars do all the planning in the church, so they program based on the needs and expectations of other stars. They like lots of singing, study, and socializing. So that's what the church offers. Stars never even consider the needs of the scrubs, because they can't relate to a person who lacks basic churchgoing skills.

So Joey makes excuses. Church is boring. It's irrelevant. It's full of hypocrites. It just doesn't work for him. Christ has a mountain for every man to climb, but Joey misses this great adventure because he finds base camp (the local church) so baffling.

⚓ **WHY MEN PREFER SITTING ON THE BENCH** ⚓

Now, back to Peg's story. Her man goes to church, but he's a scrub. He's a genuine Christian who wants to know God, but church doesn't turn his key. Oh, he's there most Sundays, but you can't get him to do much because he knows he'd be exposed as a scrub. So he warms the bench.

Just this week I was talking with a veteran preacher who told me the story of Lou, a committed Christian man who never attended adult Sunday school. When the preacher asked him why he wouldn't come, Lou reluctantly admitted, "I might be called on to read aloud, and I'm a slow reader." The preacher asked Lou, "If you were certain you wouldn't have to read aloud, would you come?" Lou answered, "With my luck, there would be a guest teacher, and I'd have to read anyway." So crippling was his fear that Lou avoided Sunday school the rest of his life.

Lou was a scrub who loved the Lord. His faith in Jesus drew him to church, but he was afraid to take another step because he didn't want people to know he was incompetent.

This is the same reason Christian men are reluctant to pray aloud, attend Bible studies, teach Sunday school classes, and so on. They're scrubs, and they're embarrassed for others to know it.

How to get scrubs into the game

Some men are different. A few are able to conquer their many fears and follow Jesus, despite the fact that they're scrubs. Some men are so drawn to God their scrubbiness doesn't seem to matter. I applaud these fellows.

But even genuine Christian men get discouraged when the stars outshine them. They get tired of being outscored and outplayed. They stop showing up for practice and eventually quit the team.

Think about this: what if we mixed up our church routines so more scrubs could get into the game? What if our pastors and church leaders began figuring out ways for the less verbal, less studious, less sensitive people to win?

Give a man a chance to use his gifts, however, and he quickly becomes a star. Central Baptist Church in Livingston, Texas, sponsors a men's chainsaw team. Each man buys and maintains his own saw. Whenever a hurricane, flood, or ice storm strikes, the men rush to the scene to cut fallen timber until power is restored and homes can be reoccupied.

We need scrubs in church. I suspect the apostles were mostly scrubs. After all, Jesus called them *dull* and *unbelieving*. Yet Christ bet the future of His church on these twelve men "of little faith."

⚑

WILL PEG'S MAN ever get off the bench and get into the game? Probably not. He has known for years he is not cut out for the Christian life. In fact, he knew it by age ten. We'll examine how the church declaws its young lions in our next chapter.

YOUR TURN

1. Do you feel more like a scrub or a star in church? Why?

2. Do you believe incompetence is a man's greatest fear? Why or why not?

3. How does a man deal with feelings of inadequacy?

4. Do you know a man who's a star in church? Is he verbal? Studious? Sensitive?

5. Think of a man you're praying for. Is he a potential scrub or a potential star? Would his natural skills and personality allow him to soar in a church setting?

TAKE ACTION

Gather a few other women and wrestle with this question: How did *verbal*, *studious*, and *sensitive* become key churchgoing skills? Is this what Jesus intended?

FIVE

How We Lose Most of Our Boys

It is no secret that worship services do a poor job transmitting faith to children in general—and to boys in particular. How has the church responded? With a flashing midway of specialized programs for the young: Sunday school, vacation Bible school, AWANA, CCD, confirmation classes, RAs and GAs, and youth group. Step right up, kids, and meet the *amazing* Jesus!

Despite this blizzard of programs aimed at youth, at least seven out of ten boys who are raised in this system leave the church during their teens and twenties.[1] If it weren't for marriage and wives to drag them back to church, many of these men would be lost for good.

What is wrong with boys?

Maybe there's nothing wrong with our young men. Maybe they're falling away because of the way we're raising them in the faith. Could our Sunday schools be unintentionally setting up boys for failure?

 **"MY SON HATES SUNDAY SCHOOL"**

It was after nine o'clock, and Susan's backyard was cloaked in darkness. Several women began pulling on jackets to fend off a light chill.

It had been an evening of support, grace, and healing. The glass patio tabletop was spotted with tears.

"I'm so happy to finally talk about this," said Lynette, a woman whose husband refuses to set foot in a church. Mitzi shared her struggles as a single woman seeking a godly man for companionship and romance. Tanya wept for her father. "I really love my dad, but he thinks church is just a bunch of hypocrites."

Sandy had been silent most of the evening. But she finally spoke with the anguish of one freshly wounded. "Just last Sunday, my sixth grader, Connor, said he hates going to Sunday school and never wants to go again." She paused to gather herself. "I've met with his Sunday school teacher, and she's wonderful. She's very bright and creative. They use a Bible-based curriculum. All of his friends are in the class."

She paused again, this time for nearly a minute. "I remember the day Connor gave his heart to the Lord when he was six. I just can't figure out why he suddenly turned from the things of God."

 BORN TO LOSE?

Why does Connor hate Sunday school? Even Connor doesn't know. After all, twelve-year-old boys are not practiced at the art of self-analysis.

Speaking as a former twelve-year-old boy, let me offer a theory: Connor is frustrated because, no matter how hard he tries, he cannot win in Sunday school. And boys must have a chance to win—or they become discouraged and give up.

"Win" in Sunday school? As a woman, this may be a foreign concept to you. You didn't realize it was a competition, did you?

With guys, everything is a competition. And here's the kicker: generally, men will only compete at things they're somewhat good at. If they have no chance of winning, they give up.

One time I tried golf. You've heard of Tiger Woods? Well, I spent most of my time *in the woods* looking for my ball. I have no knack for the game, so after a few rounds I put away my clubs. I knew I'd never be any good at golf.

That's how Connor feels. After twelve years of nursery, pre-school, and Sunday school, he knows he'll never really be good at church. It's dawning on him that he is destined to be a scrub. To learn why Connor feels this way, let's rewind about five years.

 ## THE SIX-YEAR LOSING STREAK

Connor is a first grader. He's having trouble sitting still while his Sunday school teacher, Mrs. Lennon, tries to teach the class about Balaam and the talking donkey. Connor is bored and starts making donkey noises. The other kids think Connor is funny. Mrs. Lennon does not. She finally remands the disruptive boy to Mrs. Karl, the Sunday school superintendent. Connor spends the rest of the hour alone, playing with an ancient flannelgraph in the storage closet. (Connor sets Jesus to dive-bombing the disciples as they walk along the Sea of Galilee.)

On to second grade. Connor is supposed to be coloring a picture of Daniel in the lions' den. But instead, he's folded his paper into an airplane, which makes a perfect crash landing in Loretta Jenkins's ponytail. Connor and his friends are amused. Their teacher, Miss Ramirez, is not.

In third grade, Mrs. Carroll passes out well-worn King James Bibles to every student and then assigns each a passage to look up. Connor has the misfortune of drawing Daniel 1:1. As each student reads his or her verse, a pattern emerges: the girls are better than the boys at reading aloud. When Connor's turn finally comes, he's sweating with fear.

"In-the-third-year-of-the-reign-of-king—Jeh—Jeh-o—"

"Jehoiakim," says Mrs. Carroll.

"Jehoyakeem king-of-Ju-dah-came—Neb—Nebu—"

"Nebuchadnezzar."

"Nebu-kanezzer-king-of-baby-lawn."

The other kids titter. Mrs. Carroll shoots them a withering stare. "That's *Babylon*. Please continue, Connor."

In fourth grade, Connor's teacher, Mrs. Wilson, passes out those same Bibles. She teaches the youngsters a new game: sword drills. Mrs. Wilson barks out a Bible reference, such as "First John 4:7–8. Go!" Bibles flip open; pages and fingers fly. The first student to find the passage jumps up and reads it to the rest of the class. You can probably guess which gender usually jumps first.

Connor usually likes competition, but he's not very good at this game. It combines two of his weaknesses: reading aloud and fine motor skills. Girls often read better than boys and do so at an earlier age. And throughout their lives, women have greater finger dexterity than men. Connor's clumsy boy fingers aren't very good at flipping through fine onionskin pages. One time he thought he found a verse, but he read from John's Gospel instead of John's first epistle. Disqualified.

In fifth grade, Connor is assigned the role of a wise man in the Sunday school Christmas pageant. He has to wear a fake beard and sing a solo. Connor is chosen because he's one of the few boys who still attend Sunday school regularly. Connor feels like a fool wearing a towel over his head and dyed cotton balls on his face. Somehow he manages to get through his part, delivering his lines with the enthusiasm of a convict headed for the gallows.

So by sixth grade, Connor is tired of Sunday school. He's tired of being outshone by the girls. He's tired of being embarrassed. Sunday school makes him feel dumb. Connor would rather do the things he's good at, like running around on a soccer field, kicking a ball.

That's where more and more Connors can be found on Sunday morning. Sports leagues are taking over the time slot traditionally occupied by church. This is fine with boys. They know how to win on the athletic field. But in Sunday school, it's very hard for boys to win.

⚑

THINK ABOUT THE behaviors we value in Sunday school. A good Sunday school student is one who can sit quietly, read aloud, memorize verses, and look up passages in the Bible. A star pupil is also compliant, empathetic, and sensitive. A long attention span and the ability to receive verbal input from a female teacher also help.

How many ten-year-old boys do you know who fit this description?

Oddly enough, there is a boy like this in Connor's Sunday school class. Brian is a quiet, obedient kid. He's a bit of a nerd. Brian is very studious and loves to read. He grew up in a devout home, so he knows his Bible. Brian is not particularly athletic; he's more the artistic type. He's kindhearted and empathetic. Brian is very close to his mom.

Fast-forward thirteen years. Brian graduates from seminary and becomes a pastor.

⚒ IT'S NOT JUST A SUNDAY SCHOOL PROBLEM ⚒

As you can see, there's a very good reason most boys drop out of church in their teens. Boys hate to be outshone by girls, but that is the norm in Sunday school. The more athletic and aggressive the boy, the more likely he is to lose.

The same thing is happening in our public schools. *Newsweek* and *USA Today* have written cover stories on the boy education gap. Young men are falling behind young women in writing skills. They are twice as likely as girls to be diagnosed with a learning disability.

Boys form a strong majority in special ed classes. Today, nearly twice as many boys say they don't like school, compared to 1980.[2] It's clear that females are often more comfortable in a classroom. Yet we use a classroom model to transmit the faith to boys. No wonder they are leaving us.

JESUS VS. ARNOLD SCHWARZENEGGER

Then there are the pictures.

Traditional holy pictures have portrayed Jesus as thin, pale, and soft, with long, flowing tresses caressing an androgynous face. He bears little resemblance to the rugged Judean carpenter who possessed the strength to drive out the money changers with a whip. Catholic boys meet Jesus at His weakest moment: half dead, stripped, head down, and nailed to a cross. (Meanwhile, the female icon, the Blessed Virgin, always looks healthy, calm, and serene. Hmm.)

Sunday school Jesus was traditionally drawn with a serious expression on His face. But a few years ago publishers of Sunday school curriculum realized they could sell more books to women if Jesus looked friendlier. So today's classroom Jesus is drawn as a smiling man in a gleaming white dress. He looks tidy, happy, and nice. An encouraging Jewish camp counselor, minus the whistle.

What's wrong with smiley Jesus? Two things: the image is inaccurate, and it will repulse boys, especially as they get older. Compare smiley Jesus to the tough guys in video games and films. Male action heroes are hypermasculine, scowling, and filthy, with sweat shining off their bulging muscles. Meanwhile, Jesus looks as if He's just come from a spa.

Which image do you think appeals more to young men?

Where did this blow-dried Jesus come from? Certainly not the Bible. The Christ of Scripture is more akin to a gritty superhero. As a homeless man, He was no stranger to sweat and grime. As a tradesman, He must have been well muscled. Like a video game hero, Jesus was a fighter who left a trail of mayhem in His wake. He vanquished demons (Matt. 17:18), destroyed stuff (Mark 5:12; John 2:15), and made people so mad they tried to kill Him (John 8:59). Camp counselors don't get nailed to crosses.

 ## CHILLIN' WITH CHILDREN

Even more toxic to boys are pictures of Jesus in the company of little kids.

Go to almost any Sunday school classroom in America, and you will find depictions of a happy Jesus among little ones. Sunday school curricula are dappled with images of Christ chillin' with children.

Want to know the truth? Christ loved kids, but they were not the focus of His ministry. In fact, the Scriptures imply that He spent very little time with children. Toward the end of Jesus' time on earth, some people began bringing their children to Him. The disciples tried to put a stop to it (Matt. 19:13–15). Reason with me: if it had been Jesus' custom to spend lots of time among tots, why would the disciples have tried to shoo them away? I'll say it again: Jesus loved children. However, He did not build His church upon them. The Sunday school pictures seem to indicate otherwise.

After a decade of seeing images of Jesus hanging out with the under-ten set, boys get this message loud and clear: *Jesus is for kids.* This is fine for girls, but it's deadly for boys. Let me explain.

From time to time I find myself on a college campus. It's fun to visit the dorm rooms of boys and girls and see the differences. Girls often build a little shrine to their childhood; baby pictures, a favorite stuffed animal, hair ribbons, and dolls frequently adorn their quarters. But boys' rooms tell a different story. There's absolutely no evidence that boys ever had a childhood. There's not a LEGO, Tonka truck, or Teenage Mutant Ninja Turtle within miles of the boys' dorm. Instead, the walls are covered with images of fast cars, ripped athletes, alcoholic beverages, and bikini-clad models.

Women celebrate their childhoods for a lifetime. But men strain toward maturity, anxious to put childhood behind them. What did the apostle Paul say? "When I was a child, I spoke as a child, I understood as a child, I thought as a child; but when I became a man, I put away childish things" (1 Cor. 13:11).

So, when a boy begins to consider himself a man, he puts away childish things. And Jesus is one of the first things he puts away. Turning your back on Christ and the church has become a rite of passage among boys. It is a sign of being grown up.

How do boys get the false impression that being Christlike is a childish pursuit? We tell them so. Every Sunday at 9:45 a.m.

✦ The truth about Sunday school ✦

So what's a woman to do? If you're a Sunday school teacher or superintendent, we need to talk.

I want you to know I appreciate your hard work and your devotion to your students. However, you must realize that Sunday school as it is currently done in most churches pretty much guarantees that boys will lose interest during their teens and twenties. You are a part of a system that's at least partially responsible for the spiritual shipwreck of millions of boys.

Ouch. Are you offended by that last sentence? Don't be. Instead, take action. You have the power to build your boys into soldiers for God's kingdom, instead of preparing them to go AWOL as teens.

A NEW VISION

The church I attend did away with traditional classroom-based Sunday school. Starting in first grade, we gather all the kids in a large room for fun, kinetic songs, games, and a fast-paced video that teaches a spiritual truth. Then the boys go with a male teacher, while the girls go with a female teacher. The lesson is brief (about fifteen minutes). The students sit on the floor with their teacher, who asks lots of questions. Needless to say, the boys prefer this to the usual classroom experience.

If you teach in a traditional Sunday school, make sure you give the boys an opportunity to shine in class. Let them be rowdy and goof around (at least part of the time). Keep the talking part of the lesson concise. Bring in gooey and gross things to illustrate your points.

Curt Hammill teaches a third- and fourth-grade boys' Sunday school class at Burke Community Church in Virginia. He doesn't just teach from a book; he involves his boys in the biblical narrative. For example, he once taught his class about Paul's shipwreck in Acts 27 using cargo (empty boxes), masts (poles and sheets), a plastic sword, and a real storm (electric fans and spray bottles). As he read the story, the boys acted out each part, tossing cargo overboard, doing depth soundings, and so on. As the storm intensified, Curt turned up the fans and increased the number of spray bottles.

Another boring Sunday school lesson? No way. The boys exploded from the classroom like a herd of charging buffaloes, cheeks still glistening from "sea spray." They couldn't wait to tell their parents about Paul's shipwreck.

Curt has even figured out a way to get the boys to pray at the end of class. Everyone gets in a circle and puts one hand in the middle, like a pregame football huddle. The boys offer brief prayers, then it's one-two-three *break!* Young guys like praying this way.

⌐ MAKE IT A GUY THING ⌐

Here's a no-brainer: assign boys to male teachers. Like millions of boys, Connor never had a male Sunday school teacher, reinforcing the common perception that church is a feminine enterprise. And as long as we're cruising down Politically Incorrect Avenue, I think it's a good idea to separate boys and girls for Sunday school, particularly after the first grade. That way, the boys won't lose to the girls every week. Nor will they be tempted to show off to win the girls' attention.

Can female teachers reach boys? Absolutely. But they must resist their natural tendency to teach girl-style. Instead, they should adapt their lessons to boys. Less book learning, more hands-on. No reading around the circle. Lots of object lessons. More goofy stuff. Your reward will be enthusiastic participation from both boys and girls.

And if I might slay one more sacred cow: For years we have believed that the purpose of Sunday school is to plant God's Word into children's hearts; therefore we used a classroom method. While it is certainly beneficial for kids to know God's Word, it is more important that they know *God Himself.* A truly effective children's leader will introduce young boys to Jesus—not through a series of classroom lessons, but through kinetic, hands-on learning experiences that point them to the ultimate action hero, Jesus Christ.

Y O U R   T U R N

1. Why do you think so many boys drop out of church during their teens and twenties?

2. In your experience, who performs better in Sunday school: girls or boys? Does this performance gap persist into adulthood?

3. What do you think of this idea that a classroom environment is tougher on boys than girls?

4. Do you believe the pictures of smiley Jesus among children have a negative effect on boys as they grow up?

5. If Sunday school became less of a classroom experience, how do you think girls would respond?

TAKE ACTION

Do something this week to help a boy win at church.

SIX

How the Grinch Stole Youth Group

When I was a kid, youth group was fun. It was based on three Gs: *games, goofiness,* and *God.* We sang silly songs. We played nutty games. Someone got a pie in the face. The teaching time was brief but meaningful to teens.

I loved it. So did a lot of guys. Church services were sometimes boring, but youth group was always a kick. It was the one arena of church life that was tailor-made for dudes. In fact, I first bent my knee to Christ at a youth Bible study. It wasn't a hard-sell gospel presentation that got me. Rather, it was the example of the male leaders that piqued my interest. I noticed these men were different—and I wanted to be like them. Because the youth group was so fun, I remained captured in the orbit of these great men long enough to see my own need for God.

But the three Gs model of youth group has been getting a bad rap lately. It's been relentlessly criticized for being too focused on entertainment. There's not enough Bible study or spiritual depth. The gurus tell us that today's kids are seeking a passionate, intimate relationship with Jesus.

In order to foster this passionate, intimate relationship, today's youth meetings feature long periods of singing: thirty to forty minutes is not uncommon. Youth stand in a darkened room and sing love songs to Jesus, led by a praise band of their peers. Once the singing is done, they listen to a message from God's Word presented by the youth leader.

Big churches around the country are doing this. Smaller churches wish they could. This is the new wave in youth ministry. Singing and a sermon. I call it *church lite*.

The result has been disastrous for our boys. I'm speaking from personal experience.

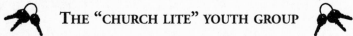

THE "CHURCH LITE" YOUTH GROUP

The church I attend in Alaska once had a youth group based on the three Gs. It used to draw 250 kids on a Wednesday night. My son loved this youth group and couldn't wait to go.

But during my son's freshman year, a leadership change brought in the new model: lengthy singing and teaching. Within a year the group had shrunk to about seventy kids. The remnant was two-thirds female. My son hung in there—but he wasn't happy about it.

"Dad, I don't want to go to youth group. It's so boring!" he said. My son has a flair for the dramatic. I thought he was exaggerating.

So one Wednesday night I slipped into the youth meeting. The room was darkened. A second-rate band of high school kids was grinding through a praise song: "Let my words be few / Jesus, I am so in love with you."[1]

About a half dozen teens were totally into it, hands outstretched in praise. Five girls and one guy, by my count. Most of the other kids sang halfheartedly. A significant number of boys were totally checked out, hands in pockets. Their body language said, *This is a drag. Get me outta here.*

The youth leader's talk started off well enough (he played a video clip from that cinematic classic, *Dumb and Dumber*), but then he talked a long time. About forty minutes. One boy sitting in front of me began snoring gently.

The youth group lost one more boy that night. I let my son drop out. I had to admit he was right. It *was* boring. There was almost nothing in that evening's proceedings to capture the masculine heart. I knew that if I forced my son to continue in this, he might be lost to Christ forever.

 ## THE EMOTIONAL HOTHOUSE

Youth groups are becoming more like this because church is becoming more like this. People expect to *feel* something at church. So we do subtle things to turn up the emotional temperature: We dim the lights. We slow down the music. We repeat verses. We repeat verses. We repeat verses. We offer more time for sharing. We describe Jesus as a man who wants a passionate, intimate relationship with us.

Girls love this. What teenage girl doesn't want a passionate, intimate relationship with a man who loves her? And once in a while a boy breaks down and cries. He has a powerful encounter with Jesus.

We think, *Hallelujah! We've found the way to reach kids.* So we turn up the emotions a bit more. More singing. More sharing. Girls thrive in this emotional hothouse, but most boys melt and evaporate. Before you know it, you've got thirteen girls and five guys at youth Bible study. And there's not a jock among the guys.

By their senior year, girls are 14 percent more likely to have participated in a youth group. And they are 21 percent more likely to have stayed involved in youth group all four years of high school.[2] Congratulations. We've set the stage for the female-heavy church of the future.

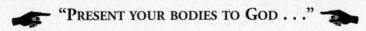

"Present your bodies to God . . ."

Why is a church lite youth group so injurious to most boys? It is a very sedentary experience; It requires a lot of singing, sitting, and listening and it is designed to stimulate the mind and emotions, leaving the body out of the equation.

What's wrong with this? Boys are kinetic creatures. Young men need to move. During their teens, boys' bodies are awash in testosterone. It makes them aggressive, risk taking, and fidgety. Healthy kinetic activity is one of the keys to unlocking a young man's heart.

Think about how the great men of God found their missions. Moses walked up the mountain. Jacob wrestled with God. David slew Goliath. Jesus plunged into the wilderness. A man's pursuit of God is often a physical experience as much as a mental one.

Paul Hill, David Anderson, and Roland Martinson are authors of an extensive study of the spiritual lives of young men. They found that young men's "quest for identity and spirituality is kinesthetic—experienced through their bodies as much as their minds. With only a few exceptions, this was true regardless of race, class or context for the young men in our study."[3]

One need only to watch Muslims at prayer to understand the power that body movement exerts in the spiritual lives of men. Yet 90 percent of Christian worship involves standing still or sitting still, either singing songs or listening to a teacher. So unless a young man is studious, sensitive, or musical, he'll probably find a church lite youth group boring—because his body is not moving enough.

Also, the lyrics of many of today's praise songs are boy repellent. Unlike the hymns of old, with imagery that included battle and blood, modern worship songs focus on our love relationship with Jesus. And we're supposed to express that love in romantic terms. Such lyrics sound odd flowing from the mouth of a man.

Picture two male hunters sitting in a duck blind, shotguns resting in their laps. The two are very close friends. One hunter decides to express his affection for the other, using lines lifted from some popular praise songs. He turns to his friend and says, "Hey buddy . . .

I'm living just to fall more in love with you

I long for your embrace

Beautiful one I adore

Your fragrance is intoxicating in this secret place."[4]

Ladies, I can't imagine saying these words to another man, especially a man carrying a loaded shotgun.

Lovey-dovey praise songs force a man to express his affection to God using words he would *never, never, never* say to another guy. Even a guy he loves. Even a guy named Jesus.

The Bible never describes our love for God in such erotic terms. The disciples did not follow Jesus because of His intoxicating fragrance. The men of Scripture loved God, but they were never *desperate for Him* or *in love with Him.* Our young men are looking for a male leader—not a male lover.

⚓ HOW MEN OFFER PRAISE ⚓

So the songs are too wimpy for teenage guys. Is the answer to make the songs manlier?

Well, that can't hurt. But the bigger question is this: if it's so hard to get young men into church, why are we spending our precious time having them sing? Is this really how young men connect with God?

You may be thinking, *Well, young men just need to learn to praise the Lord.* That is such a cop-out. It reveals our ignorance of the masculine soul.

Men offer their praise all the time. It pours out of them naturally in the right circumstances. You don't have to drag praise out of a

NASCAR fan when his driver takes the lead on the final lap. Acclaim gushes from a football player applauding his coach or a soldier lionizing his commanding officer. Men pay ten bucks to sit in a theater and worship big-screen heroes.

Here's my point: men offer their praise wholeheartedly in response to something great. An unexpected victory. A mighty deed. A wrong righted.

The problem with boys and praise music is this: young men haven't experienced much spiritual victory yet. There's nothing to respond to. So they feel strange offering gratitude for battles not yet won.

Still, we stick to our guns: *young men need to learn to praise the Lord.* So we force it. Trying to make the typical teenage boy sing praise songs is like trying to make a pig knit. Asking him to stand in a darkened room for twenty-five minutes, singing songs of appreciation he doesn't feel is pointless at best. At worst, he feels somewhat defective. He mouths the songs, but his heart isn't in it. In the front row, a handful of stars lift their palms, sway, and weep. He secretly wonders, *Is there something wrong with me? Why don't I feel the way they do?*

It's a puzzle. Most of today's worship songs are written and sung by men. And yes, some boys dig these tunes. But I'm asking you to consider the needs of the majority of boys, not just the ones playing in the band or sitting on the front row.

 **OFF TO COLLEGE, OUT OF CHURCH**

The trickle of boys leaving church during high school becomes a torrent during the college years.

We all know about boys ages eighteen to twenty-five. It's the time of binge drinking, illicit sex, and addictions of every type. Young, single men are the demographic least likely to populate the pews (just ask the young, single women). In many ways, the evil one seems to have the upper hand during a man's early twenties.

Fortunately there are still some collegians following Jesus. I met some one pleasant evening as I was standing outside a hotel in Denver. I noticed some clean-cut young adults playing Frisbee in the parking lot. Since I'm young at heart, I asked if I could join them.

Between throws, I came to find out they were with Campus Crusade for Christ, training for mission service. I asked if they'd ever served on a foreign mission team. All of them had. Then I asked, "Were there more boys or girls on your teams?" The response: *always more girls.* One boy said, "I just got back from a mission trip to Eastern Europe. We were a team of fourteen, and I was the only guy."

The spinster missionary is alive and well and living in Albania.

Christian colleges are becoming convents. My alma mater, Baylor University, the world's largest Baptist college, admitted a freshman class this fall that was 62 percent female. Camerin Courtney writes, "A male coworker recently told me about a college visit he made with his teenage daughter. Apparently she ruled out the Christian campus they were checking out when she discovered the female-to-male ratio is two-to-one. Sadly, this isn't an uncommon phenomenon for Christian colleges."[5]

WEEDING THEM OUT OF CHURCH AS BOYS

Christ left us a dangerous and demanding mission. It's a natural for young men. Yet the majority of our young disciples are women, because our Sunday school and youth groups eliminate most of the masculine boys during their teens.

By focusing so much on feminine values, strengths, and expression in Sunday school and youth group, we're preselecting the church of the future. The only boys who make it through this spin cycle are the ones whose skills and personalities match the profile (verbal, studious, or sensitive). A few others survive thanks to the intentional discipleship efforts of courageous older men. But the most masculine, aggressive, and athletic boys ages eighteen to twenty-five are long gone. Single women wonder, *Where have all the good Christian men gone?* We weeded them out of church as boys.

ꝑ

IT'S NOT TIME to panic—it's time to pray. Remember, God loves boys and men—even the ones who sleep in on Sunday. The next section of our book will show you what men are looking for—and how you can help them find it in the local church.

Y O U R   T U R N

1. Studies indicate that more than 70 percent of boys who are raised in church abandon it during their teens and twenties. Is this figure higher or lower than you expected?

2. How do you feel about long, extended sets of praise and worship music? How about the men you know? Do some of the songs seem too lovey-dovey to you?

3. Is the author trying to get us to pander to men and boys? If we turn more to boys' tastes, what might happen to our youth groups? Would the girls leave?

4. The author says men automatically offer praise in response to great and mighty deeds. When have you seen this kind of praise on display from the men in your life?

5. Regarding praise singing in youth meetings, should there be more of it, less of it, or is it just about right? What could be done to make it more engaging to boys, or should we devote that time to something else?

TAKE ACTION

Go to your church's youth group. Assess its boy-friendliness quotient.

PART TWO

A Prescription for the Local Church

For more than two weeks, my mother-in-law lay motionless. Her room was quiet, save the rhythmic clicking of the respirator. She had so many wires and hoses attached to her, she looked like a V8 engine.

Martha Jane was in a coma. She'd suffered a major heart attack three Sundays before. The woman had barely survived the airlift from her hometown of Valdez to the hospital in Anchorage. The coronary care team fixed her heart problem but couldn't wake her after surgery.

Believe me, they tried. Her room was visited by a parade of caring professionals. They brought in the best equipment. They used various drugs, treatments, and therapies. But nothing could wake her. And her health was deteriorating.

My father-in-law prayed, and then he made a crucial decision. He called a longtime family doctor and asked him to supervise Martha Jane's recovery. Even though this man was not a coma expert, my father-in-law trusted his judgment.

At first the ICU staff was surprised at this decision. But they stepped back and let the doctor do his work. He changed her treatment, removing any drug that might have a tranquilizing effect.

Almost instantly her condition improved. Four days later she opened her eyes. Martha Jane is still with us today.

☙

THE MEN OF our nation are in a spiritual coma. Even the blokes who find their way to church on Sunday are barely awake. We hire caring religious professionals who try various therapies. But these so-called remedies are having an unintended side effect—they're tranquilizing our men. Here's the sad truth: bringing a man to church may do more harm than good, for all the reasons we learned in our first six chapters.

We need to call in a new doctor. Some call Him the Great Physician. Others simply call Him Jesus.

But we can no longer stand in His way. We must step back and allow the Physician to do His work. He must have complete liberty to change our religious prescriptions. Even those we hold most dear.

The next six chapters will be a demanding read, especially for women who love church as it is. As you read on, here is my challenge to you:

Let go. Tell God you are willing to step aside and let Jesus do whatever He wants in your life—and the life of your congregation.

Keep an open mind. Be willing to consider the options as we explore what a male-friendly church might look like.

Commit. Help your church become a place where men and boys can find the Savior.

☙

BEFORE WE EMBARK, would you like some good news? The Doctor is in. There are a few churches that have freed the Great Physician to work in the hearts of men. These congregations have discarded the old religious therapies. They are beginning to see men awakening from the dead, spiritually speaking.

So what do these man-friendly churches look like? What do women think about them? How can your church become an ICU where Jesus heals men?

SEVEN

The Kinds of Churches Men Love

The Civil War was over, but the battle to connect the Atlantic and Pacific was in full swing. Two railroad companies—one building east from California, the other building west from Nebraska—vied to offer the first transcontinental link. Their rivalry was so intense that they surveyed and graded a route right past each other. It took an act of Congress to force the railways to link up at Promontory, Utah, on May 10, 1869.

In the same way, men and the church are laying their tracks right past each other. Men pour their lives into their careers, their hobbies, and their addictions. Their greatest energies go into kingdoms of hay and stubble. Meanwhile, the church creates liturgies, writes songs, and develops programs that are mind-numbing to most men. It uses a teaching style that men don't understand. It presents a soft, gentle Jesus who comforts the hearts of women and children but causes men to jump the tracks.

Not all churches are building past men, however. Some are intentionally building on a masculine foundation. Others are instinctively creating an environment where men (as well as women) are finding their place in God's kingdom.

In this chapter, we identify twelve characteristics of a man-friendly church. Using the latest research, we'll discover which kinds of congregations do the best job linking up with the male half of humanity.

⚓ Twelve Marks of a Man-Friendly Church ⚓

Before I begin, allow me to make a clarification. As I describe the kinds of churches that reach more men, you may think, *Well, I know my man, and he would never go to a church like that.*

Verily I say unto thee, there are many different kinds of men. They respond to different stimuli. It would be impossible to create a church that satisfies every male on the planet. However, studies have clearly identified the kinds of churches that have the most success bringing men in and keeping them on track.

If you're seeking a fellowship where the men are alive, look for a church that matches these twelve characteristics.

1. Look for a Large Church.

The larger a church becomes, the smaller its gender gap. Churches that draw thousands on a weekend are the most likely to approach gender balance. Meanwhile, the statistically average church of fifty to one hundred is the size most likely to experience a shortage of men.[1]

Large churches have many advantages. Foremost is *quality.* Most are led by gifted pastors who are compelling speakers. The music is polished. The facilities and grounds are well kept and impressive. Men can invite their friends without fear of embarrassment, confident that the service will proceed with professionalism and good taste. Men are less likely to leave a large church thinking, *Well, that was cheesy. What a waste of my time.*

Women often dislike the impersonal feel of a large church, but men may see anonymity as a benefit. A guy can attend a large church for months or years without ever feeling hounded to become more involved. Once a man decides to dive in, large churches offer a smorgasbord of opportunities, many of which are specifically geared toward males.

Big churches speak the language of productivity, goals, and growth. They're known for launching large projects and bold initiatives that capture the male imagination. Large congregations are often innovative. And they're usually in a building campaign, which is another area where men engage.

2. Look for Nondenominational.

For decades, nondenominational churches have grown, while name-brand churches have shrunk—both liberal and conservative. There is a disagreement as to why this is happening, but there's little doubt about who's leading this exodus: men. The National Congregations Study of 1998 found that denominational churches were much more likely than nondenominational ones to report a significant gender gap.[2]

3. Look for Strict Adherence to Scripture.

I've heard it said that men have an instinctive BS detector. Men want proof. They're natural skeptics. They not only want to know what to believe, but why to believe it.

Women, on the other hand, tend to adopt a broader palette of beliefs. For example, women—even those who go to church—are more likely to read their horoscopes than men.[3] In my experience, a woman is less likely to see things as black-and-white. She is often more forgiving of a church whose theology goes squishy. It just doesn't seem to bother her as much as it does her husband.

I'm not saying every woman is a crystal-gazing heretic in the making, nor is every man a potential Pharisee. Perhaps there's a simpler way of putting this: men tend to put rules first, whereas women tend to put relationships first. The great debates that have fractured the mainline denominations reflect this dichotomy: conservatives (led by men) believe rules come first; liberals (led by women) believe relationships do.

Churches that attract men have a bottom line: the Bible. Multiple studies have shown that churches that hold their members to scriptural standards (particularly in areas of personal morality) tend to grow faster than those that don't.[4] The National Congregations Study found self-described liberal churches were 14 percent more likely to have a man shortage than conservative ones.[5]

4. Look for a Young, Multiracial Crowd.

A study from Hartford Seminary finds a statistical correlation between a younger crowd, the presence of men, and church growth. Meanwhile, an abundance of members over the age of sixty and a surplus of women is associated with decline.

The same study found a strong correlation between a racially diverse crowd and church growth.[6] It's not enough to preach racial diversity from the pulpit; the people in the seats must represent many tribes, tongues, and nations. Look for a multicultural congregation when trying to attract men.

5. Look for a Congregation That Is Itself Young.

Recently founded churches do better drawing males. The National Congregations Study found that churches in existence less than thirty years are measurably more effective at reaching men.

Anecdotal evidence suggests that church plants do quite well with men. As we saw in chapter 2, newfound churches are desperate to grow, so boldness, strategic planning, and external focus are part of the culture. These needs jibe with men's interests and gifts.

Also, new forms of church are enjoying some success rounding up guys. One example: Cowboy churches are popping up all over the United States. Worshipers meet in barns, sit on bales of hay, sing country songs, and enjoy a simple sermon targeted at working men and women. Some cowboy churches have lassoed lots of men—running 50 percent male (or better) on a typical Sunday.

6. Look for Energized Men in the Pews.

When you walk into a church, look around at the guys. Do they look like they want to be there? Or are they just fulfilling an obligation? If the men seem to have been dragged to church by wives and girlfriends, forget it. Find another church.

Enthusiastic men bring vigor to worship. Plus you get a snowball effect: guys start inviting their friends, who show up to see what the excitement is about. They get engaged and transmit their fervor to the next group of men.

7. Look for a Man in the Pulpit.

If you're looking for a church your man might like, improve your odds by choosing one with a male senior pastor. Churches with a female senior pastor are 20 percent more likely to experience a lack of men in the pews.[7] Why is this so? Men follow men. We'll talk more about the importance of masculine leadership in our next chapter.

8. Look for a Pastor Who Is Astonishing and Authoritative.

At the conclusion of the Sermon on the Mount, eyewitnesses said this of Christ: "The people were astonished at His teaching, for He taught them as one having authority, and not as the scribes" (Matt. 7:28–29). If you want a pastor who teaches like Jesus, find one who is both *astonishing* and *authoritative*.

As a man, I love being astonished in church. I light up when a message challenges me to think—or better yet, to take action. An authoritative teacher is one who is resolute and consistent in his beliefs. He tells it like it is, even if someone is offended. Nothing disappoints me more than a sermon that does not challenge. Even worse is a message composed of familiar religious jargon.

9. Look for Informal Attire.

For years, getting dressed up has been foundational to the church-going experience. When I was a child, no one would dream of entering God's house unless clothed in his Sunday best.

Tell me: Which gender enjoys getting dressed up more, men or women? Which spends more on clothing, diets, and cosmetics? Which is more likely to subscribe to fashion and glamour magazines and keep up with the latest fashion trends?

Throughout human history, looking good has been a characteristically female preoccupation. Male vanity certainly exists, but guys like me do well to find their comb, toothbrush, and a clean T-shirt every morning.

The pressure to look good has contributed to the church's reputation as a feminine enterprise. It has made the churchgoing experience tougher on guys, because guys don't like playing dress-up.

Fortunately, this is changing. Churches that reach men today allow their members to dress informally. Some pastors are even dropping the ministerial robe, collar, coat, and tie in favor of more casual attire.

More surprising still is a quiet revolution taking place in a few African American churches, where being dressed for church has been as much a part of the religious experience as preaching and prayer. One African American church in St. Louis changed its policy to *come as you are,* and soon its male attendance tripled.[8] Don't let a dress code become an artificial barrier between men and God.

10. Look for Modern Technology.

Men and women appreciate technology for different reasons. Women usually like technology for what it does, but men think technology is cool in and of itself.

Some friends of ours had just finished an extensive kitchen remodel, so they invited several couples over for dinner. The men were unimpressed by the lovely tile, patina light fixtures, and decorative filigrees. However, we were transfixed by the microwave. It had a mechanical louver that operated with the touch of a button. None of the men understood what the louver did, but each of us took a turn pressing the button that made it move.

Churches that reach men (particularly young men) do so with modern technology. They use slides and video during the worship service. They invest in a professional, easy-to-use Web site. Some churches distribute restaurant-style pagers to parents in case they need to be summoned to the nursery.

Of course, some folks dislike technology in church. The new wave in worship, known as *vintage worship* or *emerging worship*, drives technology into the background, employing acoustic instruments, candles, and iconography to help worshipers connect with the ancient divine. But even emerging worship uses much more technology than a traditional congregation; it's just kept under wraps.

The lesson is clear: churches that deploy modern technology will have an easier time engaging men, because men think technology is cool.

11. Look for Fun.

Why does the upcoming generation of men expect to have fun at church? Blame Phil Vischer.

Vischer is a computer animator who had a dream: a series of values-based videos—starring vegetables. He started Big Idea Productions in 1993 with "one computer, little capital and no connections." Eight years later, Vischer's VeggieTales had sold more than twenty million videos, making them one of the most popular children's video series in the world. They quickly became a staple in church nurseries and Sunday school classes.

VeggieTales had an unexpected side effect: these little videos made it okay to laugh in church. Now a generation has grown up with the expectation that church can—and should—contain an element of fun. *Gulp.*

Let me be clear: a church service needn't be frivolous, nor should it be focused on entertaining the audience. But a little humor really helps men drop their guard. The Hartford seminary study also found that a *reverent* worship climate was associated with church decline (and a lack of men). So might we assume that a slightly *irreverent* climate actually helps men connect with God? This squares with men's taste for parody and self-deprecating humor. A funny skit, a video clip, or a pastor who pokes fun at himself will score big points with men.

12. Look for a Clear, Unique Mission.

When legendary football coach Vince Lombardi joined the Green Bay Packers, he found a team that had finished the previous season dead last, with one win, one tie, and ten losses. On the first day of training camp, Lombardi walked into the locker room and held a football high above his head. The coach stared at his men and then said something completely unexpected: "Gentlemen, this is a football."

He continued by explaining the basics of how the game is played, won, and lost. The coach concluded his remarks by reminding the players why the Green Bay Packers existed: to win football games.

Why would Lombardi review Football 101 with a team of professionals? These men knew what a pigskin was. They knew what winning and losing was. They knew where the end zone was (even though they hadn't visited it much in the previous season).

Lombardi knew the importance of articulating a vision. He made sure every man in that locker room knew what his team would be shooting for. His lesson delivered a handsome return. During Lombardi's nine seasons at Green Bay, the Packers won five world championships. The Super Bowl trophy bears his name.

Men love churches that make the mission clear. They focus on the basics. *This is what our church is about. Here is our mission. Here is how you can become a part of what God is doing in our congregation.*

But this is rare. Few churches have a unique mission. Most are focused on dozens of different goals. Believe it or not, less than 10 percent of *pastors* in the United States can articulate the vision toward which their congregation is moving.[9]

So men come to church, but no one ever tells them *why* they are there. Men sit on those cushioned pews and ask themselves man-type questions: *What are we trying to accomplish? Is all this activity really achieving anything? How do we know if we're winning?*

But when a church's vision is clear, men invest themselves whole-heartedly. Why do you think *purpose driven* churches are doing so well? Men need purpose, and a church that clearly articulates a mission will be a magnet to men.

A CHURCH HE WILL LOVE

So is this the secret? Just find a church with these twelve characteristics and you won't be able to keep men away?

I'll say it again: there are many different kinds of men. Your man may hate large churches. He may appreciate quiet, introspective worship. There are men who find God in hundred-year-old denominational churches with female pastors. No single model fits all guys.

But the research is clear: the more a church aligns with these characteristics, the more likely you are to find fervent men in its pews (or, more likely, in its stackable chairs). Practical considerations like these—in concert with God's Spirit—make a church more attractive to men.

YOUR TURN

1. Do you prefer a small church or a large church? Why?

2. What is your church's mission statement? Can you say it from memory? When is the last time it was repeated in a worship service?

3. As a woman, how does the prototypical man-friendly church sound to you?

4. As you read this chapter, you were probably comparing your congregation to these twelve characteristics. How did your church stack up?

5. Is your church known for getting things done? Can you give examples of how your church is producing abundant fruit?

TAKE ACTION

Share the twelve characteristics of a man-friendly church with the leaders of your congregation. Ask them to implement at least one characteristic in the coming year.

How to "Man Up" a Worship Service (Without Driving Women Away)

One of the most famous advertising slogans of the 1950s and '60s belonged to Brylcreem, that staple of slicked-back hair grooming. For those of you who don't remember it, the tagline went like this: "Brylcreem: a little dab'll do ya." In other words, it doesn't take much Brylcreem to get the results you want.

The same is true of masculinity in the church. Sometimes it just takes a little dab of guy stuff to convince a man that church is for him. Recently, a joyful woman told me that her husband had returned to the fold after more than a decade as a lost sheep. Naturally, I asked her why he came back. "Well, the Sunday he decided to visit, our pastor used a golf club as an illustration," she said. "My husband is an avid golfer, and he said he could really relate to that sermon. He's been coming ever since."

Ten years on the run. And all it took was one good sermon with a jock-oriented illustration to bring him back.

⚑

A ROCK CLIMBER can scale a sheer cliff face if he has enough handholds and footholds. The holds don't have to be large—just frequent enough to allow the climber to get a little bit closer to the summit. And so it is in church: a couple of masculine footholds can help a man feel at home in our houses of worship.

But here's the problem: without realizing it, churches have been removing the masculine footholds for generations. Mainline churches have led the way, stripping masculine references from hymns, liturgy, and even Scripture. Bible translations are gender-neutralizing all masculine references but retaining the feminine ones. (For example, we no longer refer to ourselves as "sons" of God, but "children" of God. However, the church is still proudly referred to as "the bride of Christ.") I've already pointed out the feminine spirit of our church culture. Pastors focus more on the relational aspects of the gospel every year.

Now many of the footholds are pink. We need to put a few army-green footholds back. There's no need to turn church into a macho-fest, but we must do a better job salting the Sunday experience with elements to which men can relate.

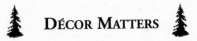

DÉCOR MATTERS

You may think that men don't pay attention to décor. You're wrong. It's not just the men with designer hair and tight-fitting shirts on home makeover TV shows who notice their surroundings.

The way a space looks and feels is very important to men, because the male brain is intensely visual-spatial. The right décor can even convince a macho man to enter feminine territory—and pay to do it. Let me show you how this principle is working in the business world.

One Saturday I was visiting my mother in San Antonio, Texas. She was getting her hair done and asked me to pick her up at the salon at noon. I followed her directions to a high-end strip mall. I glanced up and saw a pair of neon scissors in the window, so I figured I'd found the right place.

I pulled open the door and couldn't believe my eyes. I'd never seen a hair salon like this one. Hanging to my right was a ceiling-to-floor banner for the San Antonio Spurs basketball team. The waiting area featured replica trophies, autographed jerseys, gym-style lockers, and a big-screen TV flashing sports scores from around the country. Each hair-cutting station featured a personal TV monitor tuned to a sports channel.

I was in the wrong place—but I liked it.

I had stumbled into Sport Clips, a grooming destination for men. This guy-oriented hair-cutting chain was founded in 1995 by a fellow named Gordon Logan, who sensed men's discomfort with the typical styling salon. Logan reasoned that guys would spend more time and money in a place that was decorated according to their tastes. By simply changing the décor, Sport Clips has made the beauty parlor a masculine destination.

How is Mr. Logan's formula working? *Entrepreneur* magazine listed Sport Clips as one of the one hundred fastest-growing franchises in the United States. The day I accidentally found Sport Clips, every seat in the waiting area was full of men and boys. I looked at the prices—these haircuts weren't the cheapest in town. Mr. Logan is right: guys are willing to shell out a few extra bucks for a haircut delivered in a masculine environment.

Then it dawned on me. Not only will men do something girly, but they'll pay a premium price to do something girly if we simply cloak it in a theme to which they can relate.

By now I was late picking up my mom. So I asked directions (a very unmanly thing to do) and walked over to her salon, which was three doors down. I pulled open the door and the difference slapped me in the face. The first thing I saw was a quilted banner with the word WELCOME hung lovingly across the face of the front counter. The room was painted a soft pink, with silk flowers perched on Greek-revival pedestals. Four women sat in the waiting area, thumbing through magazines such as *People, O, Better Homes and Gardens,* and

Redbook. Scented candles adorned the reception table, and a decorative container of potpourri was placed beside the cash register.

Take a guess: which space felt more inviting to me?

Now let's bring this home. Tell me the truth: is your church decorated more like Sport Clips or more like my mother's beauty salon?

As I speak in churches, I notice the beauty salon motif everywhere. Quilted banners and silk flower arrangements adorn church lobbies. More quilts, banners, and ribbons cover the sanctuary walls, complemented with fresh flowers on the altar, a lace doily on the Communion table, and boxes of Kleenex under every pew.

Ribbons. Flowers. Quilts. Lace. How has this become the default look for the local church? Our facilities should resemble mission outposts, not Victorian parlors.

So what is the answer? In a word, *redecorate!* (I know that word gets you excited. Hang on: we'll cover man-friendly décor in chapter 12.)

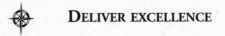

DELIVER EXCELLENCE

Men appreciate excellence. This doesn't mean slick, canned, or superficial. *Excellent* simply means done well (Col. 3:23).

But it's hard to deliver excellence every week, especially in a smaller church. Your sound system may need repair. Your lighting may be dim. You may lack talented musicians. You don't have a drama team. Your pastor is no Billy Graham. You simply can't compete with the megachurch down the street.

Relax. You don't have to be the coolest church. Just focus on your strengths and do whatever you can do *well.* For example, if you lack a strong soloist, do more choral singing. There are simple, inexpensive steps you can take to enhance sound and lighting quality. Your pastor can purchase professionally produced video clips to illustrate his sermons.

Most of all, remember to simplify. Just do a couple of things very well, and avoid anything you can't do well. Pray a lot, and leave room for the Spirit to work. That's excellence.

It seems like a no-brainer. But there's often opposition when church leaders move toward excellence. Truth is, a lot of churchgoers are suspect of excellence in church. The thinking goes this way: *If things get too professional, we start glorifying human effort. Church begins to look like any other entertainment venue, and a creeping worldliness begins to squeeze out the Spirit.*

Instead, these Christians prefer a more homespun, family-oriented service, warts and all. They enjoy hearing nine-year-old Allison play the offertory on her clarinet, even if she misses most of the notes. They don't mind a lengthy testimony from Sister Marge. It doesn't bother them when the service goes long or the pastor gets lost in his notes. These things make the service *real*. After all, we're a family of God, not some Hollywood production.

I'm not speaking against this kind of church. God has many different children, and a homespun church feels just right to a lot of folks.

But the name of this book is *How Women Help Men Find God*. I must tell you the truth: most men will have a hard time finding God in a homespun church. Research and experience back this up. Women think kiddie clarinet solos are adorable, but men find them excruciating. The brethren become impatient when Sister Marge's testimony drags past eight minutes, or when Sister Blanche stands up and asks for prayer for her aunt's gallbladder. Young men in particular are fleeing homespun churches by the boatload.

If you find yourself on a worship planning team, try to do everything with excellence. Don't attempt more than your talent pool allows. As you plan your service, ask yourself this question: *If I were a man visiting this church for the first time, would this lead me closer to God, or would it seem corny?*

I pray God's patience as you embark on this journey. There is constant pressure to place homespun elements in the worship service. A key member would love to hear her granddaughter perform in worship. The tone-deaf church secretary wants to sing a solo soon. "Pastor, I just got this amazing e-mail message. Can you read it from the pulpit on Sunday? Please?" We don't put the brakes on this stuff because people's feelings get hurt. It's easier to say yes because it keeps the petitioner happy. But over time, a lack of excellence drives men away.

Be strong. Learn to give a gracious but firm no. If you want men in your worship services, focus on excellence.

👍 FRIENDLY . . . BUT NOT TOO FRIENDLY 👎

A few weeks ago, I was a guest on a radio call-in show in Portland. A male caller told me that the reason he hates to go to church is the turn-and-greet time. He doesn't like shaking hands with strangers or having to conjure up a plastic smile and chatty small talk. On the other hand, I've heard men complain that they felt unwelcome when they visited a church and no one greeted them.

Here's another area of church life where we can't please everyone. Some churches swear by the turn-and-greet, while others have done away with it.

Let me share an idea from our church in Alaska that can make turn-and-greet more bearable for men. Our worship leader often kicks off turn-and-greet with a funny question. For instance, after a week of punishing winter storms, he said, "Turn to the people next to you and ask them how many tons of snow they shoveled this week." During a week in which Anchorage saw a record mosquito infestation, he said, "Turn to your neighbor and ask him how many bugs he picked out of his teeth this week." This dollop of humor relaxes guys and gives them something to talk about.

Some churches have taken *friendly* way too far for guys. Years ago, I attended a church where everyone held hands across the aisles while singing a unity hymn. Most men hate this—especially when they have to hold hands with other men. It's a serious man-law violation.

Huggy churches can give men the creeps. I used to attend a church that encouraged hugging. We had a sweet old guy who was a high-capacity hugger. He could lock up with fifteen or twenty people during turn-and-greet. If you happened to make eye contact with him, you were doomed. This chap just wanted to share the love of Jesus, but I'm afraid he may have driven a few men out of the church with his indiscriminate embrace.

Men generally resist the embrace of another man, unless the two are very close. Put yourself in the shoes of a male visitor who finally works up enough courage to come to church. Within minutes some big, sweaty guy corners him and starts hugging on him. What's he supposed to think?

⚓ NOW, BACK TO THE MUSIC ⚓

I've already spilled a bit of ink on the topic of music. Let's discuss some solutions.

First, a quick review of our predicament: Many of today's praise and worship songs are fine-tuned to the female heart. Some of these choruses make Jesus sound like our heavenly prom date. The concept of *falling in love with Jesus* may not bother women, but it feels weird to guys. So men sing halfheartedly, or they simply don't sing. I've met a number of committed Christian men who intentionally show up late to church in order to avoid the singing altogether. I call them *praise skippers.*

I have been praying that God will raise up composers who will write masculine worship songs. But now I'm realizing the problem goes far beyond the lyrics. A new style of singing is pushing church music farther from the hearts of men.

More and more worship leaders are adopting a breathy, eye-closing, microphone-squeezing pose that tries to wring every drop of emotion from the crowd. Worship leaders are under pressure to create the kind of *worship high* that people experience in large stadium events and revivals. Emotion in worship is a good thing, but some leaders cross the line into pop-star preening. It sounds as though they're trying to lead us into the bedroom rather than onto the battlefield.

We don't need a return to the cold, emotionless hymnody of the 1950s. Once again, the answer is balance. Worship leaders must find the courage to inject some masculinity back into the worship of God Almighty.

Where to find it? You have a treasure chest of masculine music gathering dust on the shelf. It's called a hymnal, and within its pages you'll find rich veins of masculine expression, such as "A Mighty Fortress Is Our God," "Rise Up, O Men of God," and "Onward Christian Soldiers." I encourage you to sing these hymns as written, before they were gender-neutralized. If you prefer contemporary worship, simply set these treasures of the faith to a modern beat—and listen as your men erupt in praise.

Choose "respect" songs. The difference between hymns and praise songs is simple: most hymns evoke respect for God, whereas most praise songs evoke tender love for God. We don't need to do away with all the love songs, but we must give men an equal opportunity to convey respect to their Creator. A guy will feel more connected to Jesus when he expresses his love in respectful terms rather than in romantic terms.

Lower the key. A couple of men from Wisconsin once told me, "The guys would sing if they just put the music in a lower key. But all the hymns are too high for us." Remember the baritones when you select the key.

Give men a goal in worship. Another way to connect men is to give them a goal in worship. As the service begins, tell the congregation plainly why they are singing and what they are shooting for. If guys simply knew *why* they were standing and singing for twenty-five minutes, they might participate more robustly.

Here's an example: Say, "Today we're taking on the sin of pride. We all struggle with this sin. Each of these songs was chosen to help you defeat this enemy. As you sing, give your pride over to God, and ask Him to cleanse your heart."

Given this kind of instruction, I suspect men would worship boldly. They know *why* they are singing for a change. For men, a goal is a very good thing.

Now, about that worship leader . . . One Sunday, a friend invited the Murrow family to visit her church. It was a small but growing congregation with a dynamic young pastor. The church was in the process of expanding its 1960s-era sanctuary.

We were greeted warmly, and an usher helped us settle into a well-worn pew covered with harvest gold upholstery. I was seated next to my thirteen-year-old son. Soon an impeccably groomed man dressed in a sharp suit and a multicolored necktie stepped to the podium. He invited us to worship Jesus through song, and as we did so, he encouraged us "to imagine ourselves kissing Jesus and experiencing His tender embrace."

I looked at my son. He looked at me. We gave each other a nauseated glance. I looked around at the men in the congregation. A number of them looked visibly uncomfortable at the prospect of kissing another man.

Back to our song leader. He was—how do I put this delicately?—*flamboyant.* Emotive. I guessed he was probably not going skeet shooting after church.

As I travel the country, I've noticed more than a little Elton John in today's worship pastors. This is not to say they're all gay. (In fact, that fellow who invited us to kiss Jesus? I later learned he was a married father of four.) But as I visit various churches, one constant is the *softness* many worship leaders bring to their ministry. Softness in their personalities, their vocabulary, and the way they express themselves. What causes this?

In the Old Testament, priests led worship, so you had a diversity of personality types in leadership. But today's worship leaders have one thing in common: they are all musicians. That means the bulk of our worship pastors are right-brained, artistic types. Therefore it's only natural that worship leaders are going to bring a somewhat feminine sensibility to their work.

My worship pastor in Alaska is an exception to this rule. Lee Hudson is a blues man who cuts a manly figure from behind his keyboard. He talks more like a construction worker than a worship leader. In fact, he's brutally honest about his bouts with anger, temptation, and disappointment. He goes hunting every fall, and even if he doesn't bag a moose, he always brings home a colorful story. Both the men and women of our church love worshiping alongside this man. I wish there were thousands of worship leaders like him.

Pastors and men

Men will tend to forgive a bit of effeminacy from a worship leader, if the pastor brings a masculine presence into the pulpit. But that's a big *if*.

According to personality tests, "men entering the ordained ministry exhibit more 'feminine' personality characteristics than men in the population at large."[1] They also tend to have lower testosterone levels than other men.[2]

Why is this so? Think about what the job entails. Pastors must be stars (verbal, studious, and sensitive). We prefer a minister who is caring, nurturing, and relational. In short, a successful pastor is a man who possesses many of the gifts commonly found in women.

Just last week I was speaking with a woman about her father and three brothers, all Oregon loggers. None of them went to church. Whenever she asked them why they wouldn't go, their response was always the same: "I don't respect the pastor."

Before men climb aboard, they want to see a man—a real man—at the helm. Look at U.S. politics: men consistently support the candidate who cuts a manlier figure, regardless of party. Ronald Reagan wiped out Jimmy Carter and Walter Mondale, thanks to his cowboy image. Bill Clinton won male voters with his confidence and youthful vigor. In California, Republican Arnold Schwarzenegger, the poster boy for manhood, terminated his effeminate opponent—Democrat Gray Davis—in one of the nation's bluest states. All these candidates won—thanks to strong support from men.

If you find yourself on a pastor search committee, make sure you choose a pastor with some fire in his belly. You want a pastor who speaks plainly and who shoots from the hip now and then. Hint: you're looking for a tiger rather than a kitten.

You don't have to call the Incredible Hulk as your next pastor. There's no need to release an alligator in the baptistery and see who comes out the winner. But a minister who is confident in his manhood and who projects a healthy masculinity from the pulpit will energize both men and women. You can count on it.

YOUR TURN

1. Guys will spend more time and money in a hair salon that looks like a locker room. What's the lesson for the local church?

2. Think about the pastors and worship leaders you've known. Are they more like tigers or kittens? How did the men in the congregation respond to their leadership?

3. Is it possible for a church to be too friendly? How?

4. Think about your favorite hymns and choruses. Are they respect songs or love songs?

5. I don't want to stir up grumbling, but in the spirit of constructive criticism, what's one thing your church could do to deliver more excellence on Sunday? What's keeping your congregation from doing this?

TAKE ACTION

Ask a guy whom he most admires and why.

Men Can Learn—Really!

It is strangely quiet in the temple courts. Just days ago, this holy place was a maelstrom of cooing doves, bleating sheep, and clinking coins. The man who restored order is sitting on a stone, answering the questions of a rapt crowd.

Almost unnoticed, two men join the throng, standing on the fringe, listening closely, patiently worming their way to the front. Finally their opportunity to question the Teacher arrives.

"Rabbi, we know that you teach the truth about what God wants people to do. And you treat everyone with the same respect, no matter who they are. Tell us, should we pay taxes to the emperor or not?"

First the words of flattery. Then the leading question. The Teacher sees right through their trap. But instead of blowing their cover, He decides to make an example of them.

"Show me a coin," He says. A workman digs through his dirty pocket and with some trepidation hands over a day's wages. The Teacher holds the denarius high so all can see. He asks, "Whose picture and name are on it?"

"Caesar's," the men answer.

Fixing His gaze on the spies, He crushes their plot with a word: "Then give to Caesar what is Caesar's, and give to God what is God's."

⌐

As a man, I admire Jesus' economy of words. With three simple sentences, He caught the spies in their own snare.

Jesus' parables are similarly brief and powerful. He spent much of His time teaching, and He undoubtedly preached many a sermon. But the Gospels are stocked mainly with His parables. These little stories survive to this day for one simple reason: *men remembered them.*

One time I was stuck on a long cross-country flight. I had my Bible and some time to kill. I happened to have with me a list of the parables of Jesus. So I timed each one with a stopwatch. Then I took an average. Go ahead, take a guess: how long do you think it takes to preach the average parable of Jesus?

Thirty-eight seconds.

The lessons that changed the course of history comfortably preach in under a minute.

For you trivia buffs, the longest parable in Scripture took me two minutes, twenty seconds to read (Luke 15:11–32). The shortest: five seconds (Matt. 13:33).

That day, cruising at thirty-five thousand feet, God showed me a simple truth: it is not the length of your teaching but its impact that changes men's hearts.

⌐

On November 19, 1863, two men were scheduled to speak at the dedication of the Soldiers National Cemetery in southern Pennsylvania. The first was Edward Everett, considered the greatest orator of his day.

This distinguished gentleman was an ordained minister who had served as president of Harvard University and U.S. secretary of state. He was elected governor of Massachusetts and a United States senator.

Everett, following the custom of his day, had prepared a florid speech, eulogizing the fifty-one thousand men killed, wounded, and missing following the battle that had been fought over this piece of ground. For two hours he held the assembled crowd spellbound. He descended from the platform to thunderous applause.

As the commotion died, a tall, thin man strode to the podium. He gazed out at the assembled crowd, cleared his throat, and began to speak: "Four score and seven years ago, our fathers brought forth on this continent, a new nation, conceived in Liberty, and dedicated to the proposition that all men are created equal."

Less than two minutes later, it was over. And the world had changed—forever.

The Gettysburg Address, widely regarded as the greatest speech in American history, clocked in at just under two minutes.

⚑

MY QUESTION TO those who preach and teach in church is this: Do you want to preach and teach? Or do you want to change the world? If the latter, follow the example of Jesus Christ and Abraham Lincoln. Keep it brief.

Like the orators of old, modern Christians still teach to fill the allotted time. Sunday school is forty-five minutes long? Then that's how long the lesson will be. Sermon slot is thirty minutes? Then that's how long I'll preach.

Pastor, what might happen if you preached for two minutes and then allowed the Spirit to work?

Teacher, what if you taught for thirty-eight seconds, and then let people have at it?

WHENEVER I MENTION these ideas, people are stunned. They think I'm loony. Two-minute lesson? Ten-minute sermon? People are already biblically illiterate as it is! How can we starve them with a two-minute message?

Jesus did.

There is a place for in-depth Bible study and teaching. Just not on Sunday morning in a sermon. We all know that sermons do an absolutely lousy job of equipping the saints. Thom and Joani Schultz polled churchgoers about the sermon and found the following:

- Just 12 percent say they usually remember the message.
- Eighty-seven percent say their mind wanders during sermons.
- Thirty-five percent say the sermons are too long.
- Eleven percent of women and 5 percent of men credit sermons as their primary source of knowledge about God.[1]

Why is a typical sermon so hard to remember? A University of California study found that only 7 percent of what a listener receives from a speech comes from the words that are chosen. How a speaker sounds communicates 38 percent of the message, and what listeners see communicates the other 55 percent.[2] (I suspect this last percentage is higher still for men.)

Want to have some fun? Some Sunday night, grab the church phone directory and call five friends. Ask them what the sermon was about. Then ask them what the *children's* sermon was about. Which one do you think they'll more easily remember? Which one is brief, focused on one topic, and contains an object lesson?

Folks, we're playing for keeps. Jesus told us to make disciples, baptize them, and teach them everything He commanded. But we've got it backward: we do a ton of teaching and some baptizing, but we're producing very few genuine disciples.

HELP MEN EXPERIENCE THE LESSON

Studies show that a long monologue is the least effective means of communication. What is most effective? Personal experience.

Why do you think Jesus asked for a coin and then held it up for all to see? He wanted to brand a permanent image onto hearts of the assembled crowd. You can bet that every time a denarius passed through their hands, for the rest of their lives, they recalled Jesus' amazing teaching.

Whenever you teach men, you should use everyday objects and strong, memorable illustrations so they cannot help but remember. Whenever possible, allow your students to personally experience the lesson.

One time I was talking to a veteran preacher. He was a great communicator who had built a large church. I asked him what his secret of successful communication was. "It's simple," he said. "Great illustrations. I know people aren't going to remember what I say. But all week they'll remember the stories, the object lessons, and the illustrations I bring to the pulpit. Illustrations and object lessons are like little robots that keep working in people's lives long after I say amen."

Why don't more preachers and teachers build visuals and objects into their lessons?

Pastors are not taught how to do it. Seminaries barely cover visual communication techniques. This is because seminary professors are bookworms. They have no problem retaining information from reading and lecture. They pass this academic-inspired teaching model on to their students.

The people don't demand it. John Hull wrote, "It does not matter to the listeners that they are unable to repeat even the main theme of the sermon five minutes later; the important thing is the comforting emotion of familiarity and belonging which swept over them as they were listening."[3]

Ideas for using visuals and objects are not widely available. Most Christian teacher guides do not include hands-on or visual lesson material.

It's just easier to get up and talk. People think it's hard to create visual and hands-on lessons, but your audience will love it so much that it's worth the effort.

If we're going to make disciples (especially male ones), we have to make our presentations more engaging. I challenge every Bible teacher to include a strong visual or hands-on learning component with every lesson they teach.

 ## THE POWER OF ONE BIG IDEA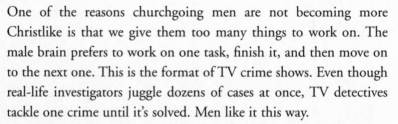

One of the reasons churchgoing men are not becoming more Christlike is that we give them too many things to work on. The male brain prefers to work on one task, finish it, and then move on to the next one. This is the format of TV crime shows. Even though real-life investigators juggle dozens of cases at once, TV detectives tackle one crime until it's solved. Men like it this way.

Consider how we teach in church. We send dozens of disparate messages each week. We expect people to make major life changes based on these teaspoons of truth.

Here's an example: Sam goes to adult Sunday school, where he receives a lesson about generosity and giving. Then he reads a devotional story in the bulletin about the power of prayer. Sam sings praise songs that focus on God's love and forgiveness. The sermon focuses on the importance of sharing your faith with friends and neighbors. The pastor quotes twelve scriptures and makes five main points.

Sam walks out of church and . . . forgets everything he heard. In truth, Sam would love to be more generous, have a better prayer life, experience God's love in a deeper way, and be bolder in sharing his faith. But his brain simply cannot work on all these things at once. So, like a computer that crashes due to a data overload, Sam locks up in spiritual neutral.

Community Christian Church in Naperville, Illinois, may have found the answer. They've adopted a teaching strategy known as The Big Idea. Simply put, CCC and its affiliated churches focus all their weekly teaching on one main theme. Every class, small group, song, sermon, bulletin insert, announcement—*everything* is focused on one concept of the week.

Men, with their highly focused brains, love this approach. You walk out of church with one thing to work on. And parishioners are taking action. For example, after presenting the big idea of reaching out to the less fortunate, one CCC group suddenly decided to cancel their Bible study that week in order to drive across town to help an impoverished church that had a need. The same message series inspired another group to perform a free home makeover for a needy single mom in the community.[4] (Gentlemen, start your chop saws.)

Think about it: what might happen in your church if men were given one clear action item for the week?

 STIR THE POT

Have you ever listened to sports talk radio? Frankly, I'm surprised that men like it so much. Sports talk radio is a raging torrent of words—with men talking on top of each other. Yet men, with their verbally crippled brains, eat these programs for breakfast, lunch, and dinner. What is it about this format that breaks through the male cerebral logjam to connect at the gut level?

It's the tone. It's argumentative. Combative. There's bragging. Put-downs. If a certain player dropped a touchdown pass on Sunday, he's barbecued on Monday. It's all in fun. Guys dig it.

Tell me, where in church life do the brethren get to argue? To banter? To brag? To fire off good-natured barbs and put-downs?

Men process truth through argumentation and give-and-take. But in the church we strain toward niceness. We are uncomfortable with conflict. We've adopted an eleventh commandment: *if you can't say anything nice, don't say anything at all.* All this sweetness and mutual agreement bores men.

Is this Christlikeness or cowardice? Jesus was so bold in His arguments with the Pharisees they often left wanting to kill Him (Matt. 12:14). Christ's fiery words embarrassed His own disciples (Matt. 15:12). Even Jesus' friends were not spared the wrath of His flamethrower tongue (Luke 4:8).

The next time you're teaching men, ask provocative questions. Stir the pot. Set two rules: (1) nothing's off limits, and (2) we all walk out of here friends.

⚔ BUILD LEADERS ⚔

I'm sick of pastors calling men to become spiritual leaders in their homes—and then doing nothing to equip them for the role. Mark Doebler decided to do something about it.

At the moment, he's in the middle of a crowd of about fifty men. Mark has called them forward at the end of the worship service for something he calls the men's huddle.

Mark is the pastor of the Grove Church in Peoria, Illinois. He ends every service by summoning men to the front for a brief object lesson that tops off his fifteen-minute sermon. He talks to his team man-to-man and usually sends them home with a touchstone, a small object that helps them remember what they've learned. This week Mark passed out pink erasers to remind the men to "erase" offenses with forgiveness. While the men huddle up front, the women enjoy some extra visiting time.

The men's huddle is cool, but what happens after church is even more powerful. When Sam gets into the car, it's not long before a little voice asks, "Dad, what happened in the huddle?" Sam pulls out his touchstone and teaches his family the spiritual truth associated with it. He hands the touchstone to the boys, who are soon fighting over it in the backseat.

Do you see what just happened? Once a week, Sam has an opportunity to be a spiritual leader in his home—because his pastor equipped him to do so.

The men of the Grove carry their touchstones in their pockets all week. Some men keep their touchstones and line them up on their dressers. These objects are tangible reminders to forgive. To love. To sacrifice.

$$\not\vdash$$

IT'S BEEN SAID that a good sermon is like a good skirt: long enough to cover the essentials but short enough to keep you interested.

Jesus taught for the male brain, and everyone marveled at His teaching. As you prepare for your next class, remember to keep it concise, visual, and interactive. Follow His example, and you'll draw men to Him.

YOUR TURN

1. What was last week's sermon about? What were the pastor's main points?

2. Could your church focus on one big idea each week? What might happen?

3. Do you like object lessons, or are they too juvenile?

4. Argumentation, give-and-take, good-natured teasing, and put-downs. Are these compatible with the gospel?

5. If your pastor were to initiate a men's huddle at the end of the worship service, would you see this as a valuable opportunity for the men, or would you feel discriminated against?

TAKE ACTION

If you are a teacher, prepare an object lesson for your next class. If you are not currently teaching, try out an object lesson on a friend.

How to Get James Bond to Go to Church

I've seen my favorite movie at least two hundred times. Let me tell you about it.

It stars a ruggedly handsome man who's extremely dangerous. He holds the power of life and death in his bare hands. He's amazingly skilled at everything. He speaks many languages. He never panics. He's always in control.

The man is given an impossible assignment. He must go undercover to defeat a well-armed, murderous enemy single-handedly. If he fails, the world as we know it will come to an end. Calamity will strike. Millions will die.

Almost immediately things go wrong. His allies betray him. Suddenly he's an outlaw. Both the good guys *and* the bad guys are hunting him down. Still, he must complete his mission. Lives are at stake.

He falls into his enemy's hands. He endures a brutal beating that would land any other man in the ICU. However, through a mixture of strength and cunning, he escapes his captor. He pulls off a series of miraculous feats and completes his mission in the most unexpected fashion. As a bonus, he wins the affections of a beautiful woman.

Men the world over love this movie. They pay big bucks to see it again and again. Sometimes the hero goes by the name of Bond—James Bond. Other times he's named Ethan Hunt, Jason Bourne, Frodo, Neo, or Spider-Man. Though the plot twists vary from film to film, the big story remains the same.

 ## WRITTEN ON THE HEART OF EVERY MAN

Why do men love this movie? It's a reflection of the big story that's written on the heart of every man. Let me tell you a secret about men: every last one of them grows up wanting to be a hero. Every boy dreams of defeating the bad guy.

Want to know another secret? This big story is simply a retelling of the Gospels.

Consider the parallels. Christ came to earth as a dangerous man—skilled, knowledgeable, and in control. He held the power of life and death in His hands. He was given an impossible assignment—to overcome a ruthless enemy single-handedly. He preferred to work undercover and told people not to reveal His secrets. His life involved a series of miraculous exploits. He was betrayed by an ally and handed over to His enemy, whose henchmen beat Him almost beyond recognition. Yet He miraculously escaped His captors and completed His mission in the most unexpected fashion. He slipped the bonds of death and defeated His murderous enemy. The world was saved. In the end, He will receive a radiant bride.

The story written on the hearts of men is the story of Jesus. But few men realize it. They go to the multiplex to catch a glimpse of the divine, when they could find the real thing in a local church.

So who's actually sitting in church, getting the mission briefing? For the most part, it's women, children, and elderly men. Where are the action-oriented guys? They're out doing action-oriented things.

Or they're sitting in the dark, eating popcorn, watching a Jesus stand-in save the world against impossible odds.

Yes, there are some action-oriented guys who go to church—and thank God for them. I wish there were more. But imagine the power our congregations would have if there were a few more James Bonds among us.

So how do we get high-powered risk takers to come to church? How can you encourage men to become the heroes God wants them to be? How can we train young Spider-Men in the making?

GETTING THE BIG STORY RIGHT

Most important, we have to get the big story right. The gospel is about a courageous man whose mission is to save the world—a man who is currently recruiting agents to assist Him in this work. But in the last 150 years, the big story has changed in our churches. Allow me to demonstrate.

What is the number one way we describe discipleship in evangelical churches today? *A personal relationship with Jesus Christ.* How many times does this phrase appear in the Bible? Go ahead, grab your concordance and look it up. I'll wait.

(Background music)

Oh, you're back. So what's the answer? Zero. When Christ called disciples, He did not invite them into a personal relationship. He simply said, "Follow Me." Hear the difference? *Follow Me* suggests a mission. A goal. But *a personal relationship with Jesus* suggests we're headed to Starbucks for some couple time.

This subtle change in how we describe the gospel is one of the reasons our message becomes garbled on its way to the masculine soul. Presenting the gospel as a relationship does not point a man toward the big story that's written on his heart. Let me show you what it does point to.

℞

Here is a synopsis of the movie my wife has seen five hundred times.

The film stars an attractive, young, single woman who lives in an exotic locale. She wears fabulous clothes and has an amazing home (often a loft apartment in New York). She's smart, sexy, and busy. Too busy for a man.

Then *he* shows up. At first she hates him. He's loud, obnoxious . . . and undeniably attractive. Through a series of misadventures (usually involving water), fate brings them together.

He woos her. At first she resists, but eventually her heart melts, and they fall in love. They live happily ever after.

WHICH MOVIE IS YOUR CHURCH SHOWING?

If you haven't seen where I'm going yet, let me connect the dots.

Men's movies: a hero saves the world against impossible odds.

Women's movies: a woman finds a happy relationship with a wonderful man.

In today's church, the gospel is no longer about saving the world against impossible odds. It's about finding a happy relationship with a wonderful man.

If the point of going to church is to pursue a relationship, you will draw more women than men. *The End.* Roll credits.

This point is so important I must say it again: if we're going to engage men in our churches, we have to get the big story right. The Jesus of Scripture is closer to Sean Connery than Hugh Grant. Christ is a strong, powerful, and dangerous man who has an impossible mission for you. He wants to make a hero out of you. He's called you to risk your life for the mission. That's the message men crave. It's a message that's lost in today's therapeutic church.

T LET BOND BE BOND *T*

Once you have got the big story right, you need to let Bond be Bond. Treat your men like the heroes they want to be.

Agent 007 is never handed routine detective work. His boss, code named M, always gives him the toughest assignments.

Many people think the church asks too much of its members. In reality, it asks too little. Thomas Rainer studied two thousand churches and found that without exception, the churches that attracted irreligious people were *high-expectation* churches.[1] Dr. Chris Bader finds "groups that are growing in membership are the ones that require more of their members."[2]

Men are actually flattered when we ask much of them. It tells a man he is valued. Remember, Jesus asked men for everything. One caution, however: Don't just ask for a man's money. Ask for his time and expertise first.

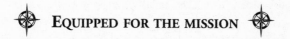 EQUIPPED FOR THE MISSION

Before each mission, Bond pays a visit to Agent Q, the wise old inventor who equips him with an array of fantastic gadgets to help him get the job done.

This is a picture of how equipping should work in the church. Our congregations are full of older men who could be discipling the younger ones, but they've never been shown how. Elders are the great, untapped resource in our congregations. We'll see how your church can utilize its wise men in our next chapter.

The unexpected

One of television's most popular secret agents was a fellow named MacGyver. He was a geeky, mild-mannered spy who refused to carry a gun. Instead, he drew on his wits to defeat his enemies. Each week this sleuth used a combination of everyday objects to escape certain death. With nothing more than dental floss, chewing gum, a broom handle, and a fire extinguisher, MacGyver could fashion a contraption that not only saved his life but captured the bad guys as well.

Men admire creativity and innovation. I think this is another reason contemporary churches attract men. It's more than just the upbeat music and the pastor with the goatee. These churches have thrown out the religious playbook, leaving them free to develop ingenious ways of expressing familiar truth.

If you serve on a worship planning team, print this word at the top of every agenda: *MacGyver*. Do something unexpected every week. It doesn't have to be grandiose. Just make a small detour off your traditional route. Put a new twist on the familiar liturgy. Innovate.

What's the first verb in the Bible? *Create*. God is first and foremost a creative being. As His sons and daughters, we have the honor of following in His footsteps. Bring a little MacGyver to your next worship service, Bible study, or prayer meeting, and watch the men lock in.

 ## Promise risk

Whenever Ethan Hunt, the main character in the *Mission Impossible* films, receives his briefing, the risks are clear. The recording always ends like this: "Your mission, *should you choose to accept it . . .*" Hunt's assignments are so demanding, he's always given a chance to pass.

He never does.

We would be wise to promise more risk to men in church. Do me a favor. Put this book down, grab your Bible, and read Matthew 10. This is where Jesus presents His mission briefing to the disciples. Go ahead and read it. I'll wait.

(Background music)

Okay. What did you think? Christ obviously flunked Church Recruiting 101. I've seen a lot of Christian promotional materials, but never one that mentions the possibility of death, injury, or loss. Can you imagine a pastor addressing the new members' class this way: "Welcome to Sunnyside Church. Join us on Sunday mornings at eleven o'clock for flogging, betrayal, persecution, and death"?

Why would Christ psych-out His team right before kickoff?

Jesus knew men. There's a certain type of man who will not give his all unless he sees danger on the horizon. But our churches are such safe, nurturing places, this kind of man does not invest himself. Instead, he takes his risks elsewhere, devoting his best efforts to building earthly kingdoms.

My home state of Alaska is full of such men. These guys don't vacation on a beach in Hawaii; they risk life and limb to go mountain sheep hunting. They spend a small fortune to fly in small planes to big mountains where the big sheep are. These men climb sheer cliff faces in the spitting snow, battling hypothermia, hunger, and injury. One misstep could send them plunging to their deaths. In fact, a handful of hunters perish every autumn in Alaska. These high-octane men wouldn't have it any other way. They appreciate the nearly impossible challenge that sheep hunting provides. Overcoming obstacles is just part of the fun.

What's the lesson for the church? If we want high-powered men in our congregations, we must do what Jesus did. Place obstacles in front of them. Promise trouble. Focus on risk—and rewards.

PROMISE REWARD

Once the mission is over, our hero always gets his reward (usually the beautiful woman). But in church, we shy from talking about reward. It seems so selfish. So fleshly. We should do what's right just because it's right. Right?

Return with me to Matthew 10. After Jesus blasts His disciples with predictions of doom, He finishes with the promise of reward:

> He who receives a prophet in the name of a prophet shall receive a prophet's reward. And he who receives a righteous man in the name of a righteous man shall receive a righteous man's reward. And whoever gives one of these little ones only a cup of cold water in the name of a disciple, assuredly, I say to you, he shall by no means lose his reward. (vv. 41–42)

Reward. Reward. Reward. I'll say it again: Jesus knows men. And men respond to the promise of reward. This desire is not sin; it's the way God made us.

Flip over to Matthew 19:16–26. Jesus encounters a rich young ruler. He's a good Jewish boy. He would be a credit to any synagogue. He is ready to follow Christ. But Jesus immediately places an obstacle in front of him: "If you want to be perfect, go, sell what you have and give to the poor, and you will have treasure in heaven; and come, follow Me" (v. 21). He then warns the crowd that it's nearly impossible for a rich person to enter the kingdom of heaven.

Right on the heels of this stunning declaration, the apostle Peter (Mr. Perfect Timing himself) decides to ask Jesus this question: "We have left everything to be your followers! What will we get?" (v. 27 CEV).

Uh-oh. Suddenly eleven pairs of eyes are fixed on Peter. I imagine the other disciples swallowed in unison. *Didn't he just hear what Jesus said about riches? The Boss is going to tear him to bits!* Judas probably started taking bets on whether Peter would survive.

But the rebuke did not come. Instead, Jesus made an audacious promise of eternal reward:

> Yes, all of you have become my followers. And so in the future world, when the Son of Man sits on his glorious throne, I promise that you will sit on twelve thrones to judge the twelve tribes of Israel. All who have given up home or brothers and sisters or father and mother or children or land for me will be given a hundred times as much. They will also have eternal life. But many who are now first will be last, and many who are last will be first. (vv. 28–30 CEV)

Jesus did not shy away from the promise of reward. He did not worry that He might appeal to the flesh. He showed us that it is perfectly healthy to motivate men by helping them understand the rewards they accumulate when they serve the kingdom of God.

Please keep in mind: we are not Jesus. We cannot promise a man a heavenly mansion with an ocean view if he will volunteer in Sunday school this weekend. Nor do I endorse the manipulative way some televangelists promise reward to those who send money.

Just because some have abused the promise of reward, we cannot ignore it. Risk and reward go hand in hand throughout the New Testament. When we refuse to point men toward eternal rewards, we reject a motivational tool Christ used repeatedly.

SERVE OTHERS . . . EVEN ON SUNDAYS

When ten inches of rain fell on Sumner, Washington, in November 2006, the community was devastated. Thirty-three homes in a senior housing park were destroyed. In response, Calvary Community Church canceled that weekend's services and sent its members into the heart of the wreckage to lend a hand.

All over the country, churches are doing the unthinkable—

canceling their worship services once in a while so their members can serve the needy. These churches are participating in a movement called Faith in Action. It works like this: for one month, pastors and teachers prepare the congregation for Faith in Action Sunday. Then instead of *going* to church, the people go into the world and *become* the church.

Think about how this changes church culture. Suddenly the key churchgoing skills must expand from sitting, singing, socializing, and sermon-listening. You need people who are mission focused. People who are oriented toward action. People who want to be heroes.

If your church closed its doors even once a year to serve the community, you'd see a few more James Bonds in church.

YOUR TURN

1. Is the gospel a personal relationship with Jesus Christ or a mission to save the world against impossible odds?

2. The male desire for reward—is it sinful, or was it placed by God?

3. How can we promise risk in church without scaring the daylights out of people?

4. Could your church, Sunday school class, or Bible study use a little less predictability and a little more adventure? How might you bring that about?

5. What's the biggest risk you have personally taken for God in the past ninety days?

TAKE ACTION

Visit the Faith in Action Web site: www.putyourfaithinaction.org.

E L E V E N

The Mystery of Male Bonding

I'm going to start this chapter with another shocking admission: in school I was a bit of a science geek. I grew up to become the artistic type (writer, musician, churchgoer). But in junior high I could have gone either way. As a seventh grader, I memorized the entire periodic table of elements—for fun.

A quick glance at the periodic table can tell you which elements will bond easily with others to form compounds. For example, when two hydrogen atoms meet one oxygen atom—*poof!*—you've got a molecule of water, or H_2O. Add one sodium atom to one chlorine atom and—*voila!*—you've got sodium chloride, or table salt. Anytime these elements get together, chemical bonds form effortlessly.

But not all the elements associate with each other. Sitting all by themselves, way over on the right side of the periodic table, are six elements known as the noble gases. They're called *noble* because they don't mix with other common elements. They are chemically self-sufficient, and they don't need anyone else to be complete, thank you very much.

For decades, chemists thought these loners would never learn to fraternize. But in 1962, a team of scientists created just the right conditions and persuaded one of these noble gases to bond with another element. Now you can find the nobles mixing regularly with common atoms—but only in laboratories, where the conditions are just right for bonding.

MEN ARE LIKE the noble gases. They tend to be independent. Aloof. They're doing fine all by themselves, thank you very much.

Women, on the other hand, are like sodium chloride. Just throw them together and they bond quickly and naturally. And church life provides many bonding opportunities for women. The beaker can be a committee meeting, prayer circle, Bible study, or choir practice. Toss women in, and after only a few weeks they become tightly attached to the friends they've made.

But men do not bond this way. Two guys can serve together on a church committee for months and never learn much about each other's personal life. A couple of baritones can sing next to each other in the choir for ten years and never get past the pleasantries.

"How 'bout them White Sox, John?"

"Whale of a game, Ted. Five runs in the bottom of the ninth! Who'da thunkit?"

 ## HOW MEN BOND

Why should you care how men make friends? Because where a man's friends are, there will his heart also be. If you want to bond a man with his church, help him bond with other men in that church. Boys who run with a pack of Christian friends stay truer to Christ's teachings. Men who walk with Christian brothers grow deep in faith, strong in service, and extravagant in love. Men who have male buddies in the church rally behind its ministry, pastor, and mission. It is truly amazing the difference a close friend or two can make.

But men have a hard time finding friends—even in church. A study by the Gallup organization found that just 35 percent of men had a best friend in their congregation.[1] A study of highly committed Methodist men (most of whom were every-Sunday churchgoers) found that just 28 percent had a close male friend who knows or supports him.[2] It's clear that our churches are not ideal laboratories for male bonding.

How do men bond? And what can women do to help? Let's approach this challenge like scientists, carefully observing how men form relationships. Then, with a combination of fervent prayer and shrewd planning, your church can become an ideal laboratory for male bonding.

Here are four basic truths you should know about men and relationships:

1. Relationships scare a man to death, but they are his deepest need.
2. Men don't usually use the word *relationship* about other men.
3. Women bond face-to-face, whereas men bond side-by-side.
4. Enduring male bonds are formed under pressure.

Let's examine these one at a time.

1. *Relationships scare a man to death, but they are his deepest need.* Many men don't see relationships as the answer; they see them as the problem. Relationships complicate their otherwise straightforward lives. Relatively few men see the benefits of a growing relationship

with God and the camaraderie of Christian brothers. So they don't bother to pursue these vital relationships, because they seem to be more trouble than they're worth.

2. *Men don't usually use the word* relationship *about other men.* In men's minds, the term *relationship* usually refers to a male-female couple. Men don't have *relationships.* Instead, they do things together. For example, if Otis wanted to make friends with Cal, he would never say, "Cal, can we have a relationship?" This would violate the man laws because the request was not expressed in terms of activity. The man-accepted approach would be for Otis to say, "Cal, let's go shoot some baskets after work tonight."

3. *Women bond face-to-face, whereas men bond side-by-side.* Masculine friendships form while guys are doing something else, such as trying to beat each other to the hoop. Or fishing. Or working on cars. Have you ever noticed when a man wants to talk, he'll often suggest going for a drive? He wants to communicate the masculine way, which is shoulder-to-shoulder.

4. *Enduring male bonds are formed under pressure.* When men struggle together, they bond. Soldiers who survive a battle are often friends for life. The same goes for athletic teammates who fight together to win a title. Fraternity brothers bond not at the party but by surviving the hangover together. Men who live through a harrowing experience often emerge as brothers. The deeper the struggle, the stronger the bond.

Remember the sheep hunters I mentioned in the last chapter? These fellows don't risk life and limb just to get a trophy; they're actually setting the stage for male bonding. High-achieving men don't open up to just anyone; they choose friends they respect. The sheep hunt is actually a proving ground upon which men size each other up. Once men win one another's esteem, they feel free to speak from the heart.

⌣↲ BONDING OVER A BOOKLET? ↳⌣

If these are the principles of male relationships, it's easy to see why men are having a hard time bonding in church.

First, there's that word: *relationship.* It gets tossed about a lot in church, but it goes *thud* against the masculine soul. In the previous chapter I demonstrated how, through a simple turn of phrase, we've transformed the gospel from a *dangerous mission* into a *personal relationship.* Every time we refer to Christianity as a personal relationship with Jesus, we unwittingly skew our message toward the feminine heart.

Men bond side-by-side, but in the church most of our bonding opportunities come face-to-face. We put people in circles and invite them to share. Some men never get used to the support group–style circle. However, there are ways to lessen men's discomfort with this format. I'll show you how later in this chapter.

Finally, are we putting men into crucibles? Are we presenting them with physical challenges? Dangerous tasks? Comfort zone–busting lessons? No, most of our assignments are academic: read this book, take this class, memorize this verse. Men will rarely bond as brothers over a booklet.

☞ THREE PROVEN BONDING STRATEGIES FOR MEN ☜

So our committee meetings, Bible studies, and choir rehearsals work fine for female bonding, but they just aren't sticky enough for men. How do we create the kind of venues and experiences that help guys bond? I'm going to share with you three strategies that can help. I've ranked them *good, better,* and *best.* Take every opportunity to steer your men toward these male-bonding laboratories.

👍 Good: Men's Ministry 👍

Men's ministry is hard to find. As I mentioned in chapter 1, experts estimate only about 10 percent of U.S. churches maintain an ongoing men's ministry.

Men's ministry takes many forms. It can be as simple as a men's Bible study group. Medium to large churches commonly offer a monthly men's breakfast and an annual men's retreat. Large churches sometimes offer a crack-of-dawn session once a week where male-oriented teaching is presented either live or via video. Many churches use the popular Men's Fraternity video series with Robert Lewis.[3] I've been through this course in a large group setting, and the teaching was revolutionary.

But I didn't make any lasting friends. Why not?

Men's ministry is typically built around a *teaching* model. We get together to learn something from a book or a speaker. Now, don't get me wrong. Men need great teaching. And men really like learning useful stuff. Men appreciate a great speaker with a powerful message.

But men's ministry often mimics the rest of the Christian life: it's another classroom experience. The lecture model cannot create the crucible men need to bond. This is one reason most men's ministry efforts fail within a year of their launch—men learn great stuff, but they do not form deep friendships.

Then there's the other extreme: some men's ministry is nothing more than women's ministry for men. Men sit in circles, read aloud, *share*, and then top it off by holding hands and praying for half an hour. Then everybody gets a hug, and it's time for cookies. If your man has the misfortune to stumble into such a meeting, he may be so traumatized, he'll never be back.

BETTER: STUFF FOR MEN TO DO

Some churches have figured out that men bond side-by-side. To facilitate this, they offer two kinds of activities: recreation and service.

A few people have always questioned the legitimacy of church sports and recreation, since they do not offer a backdrop for Bible teaching. But it's hard to argue with results. Sports and recreation is one of the few areas of church life where guys show up in large numbers. It's a chance for unchurched men to meet Christians who (hopefully) model maturity, sportsmanship, and good judgment. And recreation creates side-by-side male bonding opportunities that are rare in other church venues.

Community service can also promote male bonding, but men often shrink back when opportunities arise. I think I know why. Church-based social service has traditionally revolved around domestic tasks: feeding and clothing the poor, and caring for the sick and elderly. These ministries are vitally important, but they're not *guy* things. Life has not prepared most men for this kind of work.

But create a ministry where guy skills are needed, and men will respond with enthusiasm. Tim Doner is the director of RightWay Automotive in Anchorage, Alaska. RightWay recruits shade tree mechanics from local churches to perform free and low-cost vehicle repairs for single mothers and the working poor. Tim finds that guys who have never done much in church will gladly pick up a wrench and serve the Lord. "And once they get under the hood of a car, they'll open up and talk about what's going on in their lives in a way they never would in a circle of chairs in a church setting," Tim said.

Men's ministry, recreation, and community service can change the lives of men in ways that church attendance often can't. If you are looking to help your man grow in faith, it may be as simple as encouraging him to participate. Preferably, with a friend.

NOW IT'S TIME to reveal the absolute best way to bond men to Christ and to one another. It's a method of discipleship that's as old as the church itself, yet it is rarely practiced today.

BEST: BANDS OF BROTHERS LED BY SPIRITUAL FATHERS

Here we have the Krazy Glue that bonds men to each other and their church. This structure provides the crucible men need and keeps them from anonymously slipping through the cracks. It was perfected by a prominent early Christian named Jesus.

When the Lord started His ministry, one of His first tasks was to gather twelve men and forge them into a band of brothers. Did it ever occur to you that Jesus might have been trying to show us something? Maybe the basic unit of God's church is not the individual, the committee, the Sunday school class, or even the congregation. Maybe it's the small men's group. What if the key to transforming our world is transforming men in little teams?

Feminists, please be patient. Let me finish laying this out for you.

Think of the sheer lunacy of Jesus' method. The Lord bypassed the top draft picks, choosing instead a dozen run-of-the-mill guys. They had jobs. Some had wives. Several were foul-mouthed commercial fishermen. One was a politico. One had a problem with greed. One was a government employee. There was not a religious expert among them. Indeed, if you picked twelve guys at random out of your church phone directory, you'd probably assemble a more talented, educated group than Jesus did.

Now, what was Christ trying to tell us by this? *Structure matters.* You can gather a handful of common men, and if you weld them into a team—a true team—you can change the world with them.

How you organize and deploy your men is just as important as what you teach them, and it's more important than how talented they are.

Larry Brown knows this. He was coach of the U.S. men's basketball team at the 2004 Summer Olympics in Athens. Talk about a favorite: the Americans entered the tournament with an all-time Olympic record of 109 wins and 2 losses. They had taken the gold medal twelve times in fourteen attempts. Brown's team was stacked with National Basketball Association all-stars. But Team USA lost three of its five games and struggled to finish with the bronze.

How could the most talented players on the planet lose to teams from Puerto Rico, Lithuania, and Argentina? A sportswriter for the Associated Press put it this way: "A hastily assembled assortment of NBA stars couldn't beat a better team."

In the church, we make the same mistake as Team USA. We hastily assemble groups to study the Bible, pray, serve in the community, make music, and so on. But we fail to forge these groups into genuine teams. And men suffer for it.

FROM SCRUBS TO STARS

How was Jesus able to take a dozen scrubs and turn them into stars? He called a finite number of men into His inner circle. He took personal responsibility for their growth. He became thoroughly involved in their lives for an extended period of time. He made their development His top priority. He saw these men as His earthly legacy. Then, once they were ready, He sent them out to do as He did.

In other words, Jesus served as a *spiritual father* to the Twelve.

Spiritual father? You may have never heard the term. It comes from Paul's first letter to the Corinthians: "I do not write these things to shame you, but as my beloved children I warn you. For though you might have ten thousand instructors in Christ, yet you do not have many fathers; for in Christ Jesus I have begotten you through the gospel" (1 Cor. 4:14–15).

Paul is establishing spiritual paternity over the church at Corinth. You remember them? Wayward, rebellious, sinful. As their spiritual father, Paul is exercising his right to speak authoritatively into their lives.

Look at the verse again: "Though you might have ten thousand instructors in Christ, yet you do not have many fathers . . ." The situation in Paul's day was not much different than ours. Modern churches are full of men who want to preach and teach. But how many fathers do we have? How many men are willing to put their time and treasure at risk in order to personally grow men to maturity?

Think about your church. Is there even one man who is raising up disciples the way Jesus did?

- He takes finite number of men into his inner circle.
- He takes personal responsibility for their spiritual growth.
- He becomes thoroughly involved in their lives for an extended time.
- He makes their development his top priority.
- He sees them as his earthly legacy.
- Once they are ready, he sends them out to do as he did.

I would guess that in most churches not one man is doing this kind of work with other men. Pastors certainly don't have time do it, with all the demands we heap upon them.

A man cannot rebuild his life alone. He not only needs God, but he must also have the security and support of a small group of guys he knows and trusts. Once he is restored to spiritual health, he is already surrounded by brothers who will help him grow in faith and help him if he falls (Eccl. 4:10). This is how the church is meant to function.

HOW SPIRITUAL FATHERING IS CHANGING ONE CHURCH

This is not mere theory. Spiritual fathering is beginning to transform churches across America. Let me end this chapter with a true story.

Eighty percent of the citizens of Milwaukee, Wisconsin, will tell you they are either Catholic or Lutheran, but only 21 percent go to church. It's one of the most religious but least churched cities in America.

In the early 1990s, Elmbrook Church in suburban Milwaukee hired Steve Sonderman as the men's minister. In his first month on the job, Steve held a funeral for the men's pancake breakfast. Instead of trying to gather a big crowd of guys to listen to a speaker, Steve started discipling a handful of men. Not superstars, just regular knuckleheads. He taught them from the Bible. He took them into the community. Steve was tough on them. He set very high expectations. Being discipled by Steve Sonderman was like hugging a cactus. It was part seminary, part missionary, part coronary.

When he felt his men were ready, Steve sent them to disciple other men. He followed their progress and helped them as challenges cropped up.

Today, Elmbrook Church has some fifteen hundred men meeting in small groups all over southeastern Wisconsin. Each is led by a competently trained spiritual father (though Steve doesn't use that term). The curriculum Steve wrote, under the manly moniker *Top Gun*, is being used to disciple men the world over.[4]

Elmbrook has accomplished this without a weekly men's meeting. No auditorium filled with men listening to a teacher. No annual men's retreat. Not even matching polo shirts. Instead, the entire men's ministry consists of little bands of brothers living the Christian life in teams. As the groups proliferate, men with leadership potential are trained and sent to form new groups. The ministry grows one spiritual father at a time.

Here's the best part: a new believer can have a spiritual father and a band of brothers around him within minutes of his decision. In most churches we pray with converts, pat them on the back, and wish them well. During the next eight weeks, more than half of those new believers will disappear, never to be seen in church again.[5] But at Elmbrook, no man gets left behind.

Elmbrook Church has benefited greatly from the presence of so many committed men. The church has enjoyed a long season of growth and peace. It is now the largest church in the state of Wisconsin, welcoming more than eight thousand worshipers on a typical weekend.

Fifteen years ago, Steve Sonderman stood at a crossroads. He could have followed the usual church script: put on events, try to gather a crowd, try to funnel men into small groups. These large gatherings would have done some good. Men would have been taught God's Word. A few lives might have been nudged in the right direction.

But instead, Steve followed Christ's structural blueprint. He has birthed an army of committed men, organized in little platoons. Men who are being continually strengthened in faith, loving their families, and serving the community. Because of the masculine leadership structure, men finally feel free to sit in circles and share from the heart. Men study the Bible and read Christian books. And guess what? *They like it.*

You may be wondering, *What about the women?* Well, like almost every other church in America, Elmbrook has a thriving women's ministry. But that's the easy part. Sodium chloride, remember?

To recap:

> Men's ministry = good.
> Stuff to do = better.
> Bands of brothers led by spiritual fathers = best.

Now you know how men bond. What can *you* do about it? More than you think. We climb that hill in our next chapter.

Y O U R   T U R N

1. Will men really grow stronger in a male-only context? Or are mixed gender gatherings just as effective?

2. Is the men's small discipleship group the basic unit of the church? If so, where do women fit in? Children?

3. Dream a bit: what might happen to your church if every man had a spiritual father and a band of brothers?

4. What benefits would women experience if men were rigorously discipled by other men?

5. What impact might men's discipleship groups have on the boys?

T A K E   A C T I O N

Find out if your church offers man-to-man discipleship opportunities.

How One Woman Can Awaken
Her Congregation

My wife and I often take a walk after dinner. We review our day, plan for tomorrow, and pray. It's good for our marriage and our health. It also helps me burn off that extra helping of pasta I shouldn't have eaten.

A few nights ago, we were walking down a darkened street. Without warning, I felt a gentle hold on my leg. I looked down but couldn't see anything. I pulled; it pulled back. I pulled again and broke free.

Once we got under a streetlight, I found the remains of the snare attached to my blue jeans: a spider web. Actually, it was about a dozen strands of finely spun thread. I marveled at the power of this spindly substance to impede the movement of an adult male. Back home that evening, I searched the Internet and found that a spider's web is five times stronger than steel, by weight. It looks so fragile, yet it possesses tremendous power.

As you read the preceding chapters of this book, you may have felt a mixture of joy and despair. Joy at finally understanding the hurdles men face at church—but despair at not being able to do much about them. Don't be so sure about that. Women are like spider webs: they may think they are powerless, but they possess tremendous hidden strength. And if you bundle a dozen or so women together, you can literally change the course of your congregation.

You may say, "But I'm not a revolutionary. I like my church. Why should I try to change it?" First, we're not talking about huge changes. Many of the adjustments that would make your church friendlier to men are not hard to accomplish. Second, if you believe as I do that Christ died for all, then we need a church that makes disciples of all, both female and male.

So let's get to work.

⚓ First, spin a relational web ⚓

Take a lesson from the spider web. Don't go into this alone. If you do, you'll be quickly shredded.

Your first step should be to gather a circle of sisters. Maybe your circle already exists. If there is a group of women in your church who are focused on praying for the men in their lives, by all means, join it. If not, begin praying that God would send you a friend who understands.

Nancy Kennedy found a woman named Terry, who walked alongside her when Nancy was a brand-new Christian. Both women were married to irreligious husbands. Nancy wrote, "When I was with Terry, I was no longer alone. She understood—really, truly, completely understood. When I blew it and chased Barry around the house, nagging at him to 'just come to church once and I promise I won't ask you again,' she understood my tears of anger, remorse and frustration."[1]

Once you find your Terry, the two of you should begin building a circle of sisters. This should be an easy sell. Every woman in your church is probably praying for at least one man in her life. Spin your relational web slowly. Learn to love and support each other. (It's not only guys who benefit from a team.)

You may want to launch an organized women's group through your church. For example, one church offers a Moms Without Partners group during the Sunday school hour for single moms and those who are spiritually single.[2] Another church offers a class to equip wives to reach their husbands with the gospel. In the first three months of the class, four husbands became Christians.[3]

If you don't want to deal with church bureaucracy, you can simply invite a handful of women over to pray and see if the group clicks. Look for these sisters at church, at work, at your Bible study, or in your neighborhood.

Once you're gathered, make the purpose of the group clear. Follow the template in chapter 1 of this book. Start the group by asking each woman, "What's your number?" Be a strong leader. Provide love and support, but keep the women focused on your goal: the revival of your men. Don't let the group stray onto any other agenda.

Here is more team-building advice from Nancy Kennedy:

- Keep from gossiping. Make it a rule: no guy bashing.
- Keep it purposeful. Meet regularly and go through this book or a Bible study together. This focus will help you bond and keep women from dropping out.
- Keep praying. End your times together with intense prayer for your men. Bring their photos and place them in the circle one-by-one as you pray for each man individually. Don't rush this: allow all the women to focus their prayers on each man individually. If you do not have photos, write each man's name on an index card and drop the cards into the center, one at a time.
- Keep yourself from envy—especially if someone else's guy turns to Christ but yours doesn't.

- Keep your priorities. Enjoy your sister time together, but don't let it supplant your time with your husband and children.
- Keep it Christ-centered. Forget about what you read in *People* magazine. Stay focused on what God says.

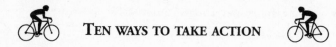

Ten ways to take action

Once you have your circle in place, you can begin to take action. You and your sisters need to become the men's spiritual development cheerleading squad. Here are ten ideas to get you started:

1. Go to Your Pastor and Offer the Support of Your Team.

Gather your sisters and take your pastor to lunch. Tell the pastor you'd like to help the church reach more men. Show him this book and pledge your help. (You might suggest he read my book *Why Men Hate Going to Church.*) As a group, promise your support as he takes the church in a more man-friendly direction. Furthermore, tell the pastor that if someone gets her nose out of joint, "Send her to us. We'll take care of it."

Your pastor will probably think he has skipped death and gone straight to heaven. A team of women who will support him when traditionalists balk is a precious gift. This keeps your pastor out of the gun sights and allows him to focus on ministry while you smooth any ruffled feathers.

2. Go to the Men's Ministry Leader and Offer Your Support.

If your church has a men's ministry, it is probably being led by one overworked, underappreciated guy. I can promise you—he needs help. Call him and offer the support of your sisters. You can help with food preparation, meeting logistics, room setup—whatever he needs. Offer to be his team of angels.

If there is no men's ministry in your church, I can guarantee there's a guy who has a heart to start one. Find out who he is (through the pastor) and offer your support. I cannot tell you how encouraging this will be to him.

3. Plan an Event to Encourage the Men.

Here is a simple but revolutionary idea: gather your circle of sisters and plan an annual Men's Appreciation Night at your church. (Schedule it near Father's Day.) Restrict attendance to men eighteen and older. Let it be known that the women of the church are sponsoring it, in order to thank the men for their faithful participation over the past year. Decorate with man stuff. And by all means, serve unhealthy guy food.

Be sure to start with a little humor—maybe a reading from that seminal text on the human male, *Dave Barry's Complete Guide to Guys.*[4] Offer a fun competition and give away a couple of prizes. Once the fellas have had a good laugh, transition to a more serious note. Invite several women to come forward to express their appreciation for the men of the congregation. Be specific. The choir director can thank her male vocalists by name. The secretary can thank two men who helped get her car started last January. Finally, three or four women can read love letters to their husbands (though don't overdo this).

I tell you the truth: most Christian laymen have never received a teaspoon of thanks for their church involvement. Instead, Christian men usually endure criticism for not doing enough. Your circle of sisters can change this. And by restricting attendance to men eighteen and older, you create a rite of passage for the boys to look forward to when they become men.

4. Redecorate the Church.

In chapter 8, I promised we'd redecorate. Well, ladies, it's time for *Extreme Makeover—Church Edition.*

But before you pull out your paint chips, take your circle of sisters on a *man safari* of your community. Visit the places guys hang out. If your town has one of those sporting goods Taj Mahals such as Cabela's or BassPro Shops, pay a visit. You might also duck into a sports bar, a cigar humidor, or a men's gym. If there is a big-game hunter in your church, he'll be glad to show off his trophy room.

As you visit each location, note the color scheme and décor. Observe the lighting and symbols. Get a feel for each space and note its layout. Take pictures if you can.

Conclude your safari by visiting your church. Look at your facility through the eyes of a male visitor. Within moments you'll probably declare a decorating emergency.

Decorating a church is not hard; it's the *undecorating* that can cause a church split. Those quilted banners that have hung on the sanctuary walls for years? Handmade by Sister Betty, who passed away in November. The embroidered altar cloth on the Communion table? Carried from the Holy Land by Sister Agnes. Those decorative flower vases on the chancel? Given in memory of Gladys Frump's father and mother.

Mess with these mementoes and you'll face growling, snapping, frothing opposition. No longer mere decorations; these accoutrements are now memorials to the saints. Taking them down diminishes the memory of those who came before. So you may have to think of creative ways to redeploy these holy relics. I wish you well.

If by some miracle you're able to move the relics without inciting violence, then you've earned the right to redecorate with men in mind. Obviously, you can't hang neon beer signs in the sanctuary. But you can do a lot for men, such as the following:

- Choose masculine colors. Look to earth tones, colors of the field.

- Use river rock or natural stone as accents (think wilderness lodge).
- Use directional lighting to add warmth.

I think I'm going to stop right here. Like most men, I lack the decorating gene. The rest is up to you. Have fun.

5. Support Man-Only Opportunities and Events.

One time I was coordinating a men's service day at our church. The idea was to mobilize the men to prepare the building and grounds for an Alaska winter and to perform minor car repairs for people in need. The preparations were moving forward smoothly—until a woman named Nora approached me and said she felt discriminated against. Nora felt she had every right to serve alongside the men. She threatened to go to the elders and ask for the event to be cancelled if women were not allowed to volunteer.

Did Nora have the right to participate? Absolutely. But I asked her to lay down that right, as a gift to the men. I pointed out that our church had dozens of women-only opportunities, but this was the one time all year that men were going to step up and serve.

Nora graciously gave up her crusade. The volunteer corps remained man-only and attracted a large crowd of guys, many of whom were the nonreligious husbands of churchgoing wives. I'm convinced the man-only designation helped swell our ranks, and it drew men on the fringe to serve.

Believe it or not, some women actively oppose men's ministry because women cannot participate. In their minds, this makes men's ministry sexist and discriminatory. This attitude reflects a distrust of men that women pick up in universities and from the media. *Men just can't be trusted. If men gather without women around, women end up being oppressed. I'd better be there just to make sure my gender is represented.*

This need to control is as old as humanity itself. In Genesis 3, God discovers Adam and Eve have sinned. He offers a lengthy rebuke to the snake and to the man, but the woman receives just a two-sentence injunction: "I will sharpen the pain of your pregnancy, and in pain you will give birth. And you will desire to control your husband, but he will rule over you" (Gen. 3:16 NLT).

You and your sisters need to help the women of the congregation relinquish control of the men. They must learn to trust men, even when there are no women in the room. Women should let the men manage their own spiritual lives (even though the women would undoubtedly do it better).

6. Let Men Do Guy Things without Freaking Out.

Women of the church can knock the legs out from under their men without realizing it, by opposing things they don't like or understand.

A men's group at a church in Florida decided to sponsor a men's paintball night. This raised the hackles of two influential women, who felt that paintball promoted war and sent a message to boys that guns belonged at church functions. These women complained to the pastor, who shut the event down. Needless to say, the men felt like little boys who'd been sent to the principal's office.

Women, it's not your responsibility to supervise the men's ministry. Give men the benefit of the doubt, and let them police themselves.

7. Support the Placement of Men in High-Profile Leadership Positions.

This is very hard for me to write, because I believe in the equality of the genders. Nevertheless, if we're going to bring men back into full participation, we must do a better job nurturing male lay leadership in the church and placing men in visible leadership positions.

All men have a disease. It's called *she'll-take-care-of-it-itis*. It's a form of amnesia. Once a woman starts taking care of something, men forget completely about it. For example, my wife supervises our children's education and health. I have only a vague notion about their schooling or what shots they need. If they get a cold or have a test coming up, I often don't even realize it. This is not because I don't care; it's because I know my wife will take care of it. My male brain can only juggle so many balls, and Gina does a magnificent job covering these bases.

Some churches are incubators for *she'll-take-care-of-it-itis*. It's not uncommon today in mainline churches for women to lead the entire service: a female pastor, liturgist, and choir director officiate, while lay women lead the prayers, serve communion, and take the offering.

When weeks pass between man-sightings, the brethren begin to lose heart. Soon you can't get the men to do anything. In the absence of men, more women step forward. The disease spreads. In times past women were excluded from leading in worship, but with so much feminine presence in mainline congregations, men are now excluding themselves.

Here's a suggestion you probably don't want to hear: it may be helpful for women to step back from leadership in the church so men will have no choice but to step forward. You may even need to set aside some high-profile positions for men.

What would justify such self-imposed discrimination? Let's put aside the biblical presumption of male leadership for a moment. From a purely practical standpoint, male leadership emboldens other men to step forward to lead. It provides young men growing up in the church with male role models. And look at the facts: the churches that have opened their doors widest to female leadership are in steep decline. Meanwhile those old-fashioned churches with men in the top posts continue to grow.

Am I saying women should never lead in church? No. But if your staff is heavily female, you'd better work extra hard to place laymen in high-profile leadership positions. Otherwise you'll suffer the fate of so many other declining churches whose men have quit or gone passive. In twenty years, you'll have a church full of old women wondering where all the men and young people have gone.

If you're a feminist, this may be a hard pill to swallow. But remember: in church, men are a minority group. Think of this as an affirmative action program that will increase diversity.

8. Resist the Tendency to Feel Offended or Excluded.

Society teaches women to feel victimized anytime men get something women don't. So if your church focuses on men and boys, you have to make a conscious decision not to play this game.

In chapter 9 I wrote about a church that added a men's huddle at the end of the worship service. The women of this congregation had to give up their right to feel left out by keeping the bigger prize in mind: a more inclusive church where everyone feels valued and needed.

9. Beware of the Female Equivalent.

As you were reading that last paragraph, you may have been thinking, *Why doesn't that church just offer a women's huddle too? Then nobody is left out.*

When women observe a successful program for men and boys, it's not long before one of them exclaims, "We need a program like that for women and girls!" Yet the launch of a female-equivalent program can hasten the demise of the men's program.

Here's how it happens: Let's say First Church launches an evening basketball ministry for at-risk boys. About thirty to forty young men show up every Wednesday night. Soon girls are clamoring to join the fun. Church leaders decide to launch an equivalent ministry for young ladies. The girls' program grows rapidly and soon eclipses the boys' league. Word on the street is that First

Church's basketball program has become a *girls' thing*. Boys start dropping out, and their program is eventually cancelled. The girls' program lives on.

As we learned in chapter 2, men don't do *girls' things*. Their enthusiasm wanes as soon as women begin participating. Now, don't shoot the messenger. I agree that this is one of the most frustrating things about the male psyche. But it's the way men are—particularly young men. Guys need experiences that are uniquely theirs. They need ministries that women cannot attend, commandeer, or copy.

Is your heart large enough to give men this gift?

10. Support Change to Make the Church More Fruitful.

I've saved the most important tip for last. Women, this is huge. We men need you to support changes that make the church more fruitful. Fruitfulness not only attracts men but it promotes church growth and health. On the other hand, pointless activity discourages men.

I have a musician friend (let's call him Bill) who almost abandoned his faith over a fruitless worship service. His church had always offered an 8:00 a.m. service on Sundays. But over the years attendance had dwindled to fewer than ten early birds. Sometimes there were more volunteers on stage than there were worshipers in the pews. Bill was discouraged by having to rise extra early to entertain as few as three attendees.

The obvious answer was to cancel the 8:00 a.m. service and convince the morning glories to join the other 150 members at the 10:30 service. But these traditionalists held on to *their service* by appealing to the deacons. Wanting to keep these folks happy, the deacons decided to continue offering two worship services and pray that the Lord would bring more people to the 8:00 a.m. service. But the Lord did not bring more people. Bill became disillusioned. He quit volunteering in the service. He eventually moved to another church.

Be honest. Church life is a basket of fruitless activity: Committee meetings that accomplish little. Ministries that do not change lives. Traditions that have lost all meaning. And pointless activity poisons men.

Now, here's the irony: women often oppose change that would help the church grow. Without realizing it, they find themselves defending the status quo. Let me show you how this happens with another true story (names changed).

Sharon is an empty nester in her midfifties. She's been a member of Lakeview Methodist Church for almost twenty-five years. Lakeview is a typical graying congregation, caught in a slow decline. So church leaders are considering a name change to Lakeview Christian Fellowship. They're following the lead of thousands of other churches that have attracted new blood by simply dropping their denominational name from the church sign. Lakeview will remain a Methodist church, but it will not trumpet that affiliation.

It seems like a simple change. The reason has been well explained. Everyone agrees the church needs to do something to reverse its fall. But there is opposition nonetheless. Battle lines are drawn. People are divided. Feelings are hurt.

Sharon has been concerned that the church is failing to attract young people, so at first she supported the name change. But now that it's created so much acrimony, she's withdrawn her support.

What made her change her mind? She still thinks the new name is a good idea. But Sharon sees the church as a family of God. Therefore, anything that divides the family is probably not God's will. One by one the women of the church are coming to this conclusion. The men are falling in behind their wives. Support is quickly eroding.

So the name change is stopped. The church continues to be known as Lakeview Methodist Church. Peace is restored. And the congregation continues a slow march to its death.

This scenario plays out thousands of times a year in our churches. The issue is not the name—it's the fact that women tend to resist change in the church because change always stirs up conflict. Many women are natural peacemakers and will do almost anything to avoid discord.

Church conflict is inevitable. Christ prayed that we would be one, but He also predicted division. "I did not come to bring peace, but a sword," He said. "For I have come to turn 'a man against his father, a daughter against her mother, a daughter-in-law against her mother-in-law—a man's enemies will be the members of his own household'" (Matt. 10:34–36 NIV). Jesus made it clear: whenever the kingdom of God advances, expect bitter conflict, even within families. Even within church families.

The most Christlike decision is not necessarily the one that keeps the peace. That's why you, as a woman, must support changes that move the church forward in its mission. Even if those changes stir up conflict. The men are counting on you.

YOUR TURN

1. In general, do you support change in your church, or do you try to stop it? Do you avoid conflict, or do you see conflict as a necessary part of growth?

2. What would happen if several key women in your church voluntarily stepped back from leadership, so men could step up?

3. When small groups of men gather, are you trusting or suspicious? Do you feel better if there's a woman in the room?

4. Do you know a man who suffers from *she'll-take-care-of-it-itis*? How does this affect his life—at church and at home?

5. What are your church decorating ideas? Share them with the other women.

TAKE ACTION

Begin searching for your Terry. Or look for an existing women's group focused on reaching men. If you've already done this, invite your pastor to lunch and offer the support of your circle.

PART THREE

How to Reach the Men You Care About

A few years ago, my daughter Andrea wanted a pair of in-line roller skates. She was angling for a brand-name set, which were priced just north of a hundred bucks. Since her fourth-grade feet were growing faster than an Alaskan jumbo cabbage, I didn't see this as a prudent investment. She persisted, so I told her she'd have to earn the money herself.

Like a good father, I sat her down and offered several ideas to raise some dough, including a number of chores I needed done around the house. Floor mopping, garage cleaning, and car washing were on the list, as I recall.

As I ticked off the docket of backbreaking labors, Andrea began to wilt. She finally looked at me through woeful eyes and said, "Daddy, is there *anything else* I can do?"

As you read the first dozen chapters of this book, you may have felt distraught. Overwhelmed. The very idea of reforming your church may have seemed too daunting. Perhaps you wondered, *Is there anything else I can do to get my men interested in the things of God?*

I stood firm with my daughter, but I'll go a little easier on you. The remaining chapters of this book deal with *everything else* you can do to enhance your personal outreach to men and boys.

What You Do . . . What God Does

Women put tremendous pressure on themselves to save their men. Linda Davis wrote:

> How often do you catch yourself thinking, "If only I were doing certain things better—loving, submitting, witnessing—he would already be a born again wonder"? Do you ever feel he won't accept Christ because your failures and imperfections are a stumbling block: "If I hadn't been so crabby the other day; if I weren't always yelling at the kids; if I hadn't run up the charge account," and so on? Do you ever blame yourself?[1]

If you've been holding yourself personally responsible for the salvation of the men you love, please stop. The first twelve chapters of this book should have relieved a lot of guilt. It should be obvious to you now that our churches often make matters worse. In fact, a man's distaste for Christian culture may be masking a genuine thirst for God.

But first, let's get something straight: even if he attends a man-friendly church, your guy may not come to God. Your witness might be perfect, yet he may not choose to follow Christ. Why? Because only God the Father can bring people to Himself. Listen to what Jesus said: "No one can come to Me unless the Father who sent Me draws him" (John 6:44). Your faithful witness cannot save him; your wonderful church services cannot fill him with the Spirit. Only God the Father can attract men to Christ.

But just because God does the attracting doesn't mean we humans have no role to play in the salvation drama. The apostle Paul made it clear that our efforts *can* help win men to Christ. Paul modified his evangelistic methods depending on the culture of his audience (1 Cor. 9:19–22). In the same way, we must take man culture into account when we share our faith.

God is after your men. The Bible promises us that He is not willing that anyone should perish, but that everyone should come to repentance (2 Pet. 3:9). God loves your men more than you do.

So the pressure is off. Relax. God is on the job.

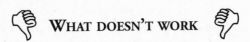

WHAT DOESN'T WORK

Some women take the pressure off themselves, but they place it right back on the men they love. They try guilt, manipulation, begging, or bargaining to get their man involved at church. Some women pout if he skips services. Others dangle incentives such as peace in the home or a favorite meal to get their man into a pew. I've even heard of a wife who gave her husband this ultimatum: "No church—no sex." Ladies, believe me, this is a losing evangelistic strategy.

Other women think emotional manipulation will awaken a man's spiritual desire. Every weekday morning, Nancy Kennedy's little two-year-old would melt her daddy's heart by saying, "Daddy go work?" Nancy noticed the softening effect the girl had on her father. So, with the aid of cookies, Nancy taught the toddler to say, "Daddy go church?"

Her husband sniffed out the conspiracy immediately, and Nancy's attempt at parrot evangelism drove her husband farther from the Lord.

Some strong-willed women simply order, threaten, or browbeat their men to church. Please don't do this. Such bullying will cause him to resent you and God at the same time. There is no value to having a man's body in a pew if his heart is elsewhere.

Women, you will make the gospel repellent if you try to manage a man's walk with Christ. If he doesn't want to go to church, Bible study, or the men's meeting, don't say a word. Let the decision be his.

 ## UNDERSTAND YOUR MAN

It's important to understand your man's religious background and experiences. Many women neglect this step when attempting to minister to the men they love. How foolish. An expert fisherman learns all he can about the species he's trying to catch. You must become a student of the man you're hoping to win to faith.

So start asking questions. Did he have a bad experience in church as a child? Is he an atheist? Is he practicing another religion? Is he held captive by besetting sin? Does he have some deep-seated bias against the church? If so, what is its source?

WAS HE INOCULATED AGAINST CHRISTIANITY?

Do you know how vaccinations work? The doctor injects a dead or weakened form of an infectious germ into a patient's bloodstream. The body attacks the sample germ, creating antibodies and granting the patient immunity from the full-blown disease.

Unfortunately, many men were inoculated against Christianity as boys. They were injected with a dead or weakened version of the faith.

This exposure was just enough to keep them from developing the full-blown disease as adults. Ask these men if they are Christians, and they'll respond, "Yes, I was raised _____ (fill in denomination)." These men carry their childhood religious affiliation like a tattered ID card, stuffed deep in their mental wallet. They may consider themselves religious or spiritual, but there's no ongoing connection to a local church. And, truth be told, there is little connection to God.

In talking to people, my very unscientific survey finds that men raised in liturgical churches are most likely to have been spiritually vaccinated as kids. Liturgy can be deeply meaningful, but it dampens spontaneity, making faith seem dead to the young. These men are stuck: they believe in God, but they won't explore a richer life of faith because they already have their religious box checked.

Other men are so-called *fire insurance Christians.* Somewhere along the line these men asked Jesus to be their Savior, but they are not walking daily with Him. The evangelist told them their ticket to heaven was punched, so they feel free to live life as they please. Still others are *balance scale Christians.* Their theology sounds like this: "God loves me. The good in my life outweighs the bad, so He will let me into heaven."

It's very hard to infect a vaccinated man. How do you get past his religious defenses to help him see his need for Christ? Just make sure he knows what God is up to—in your life and in your church. As he meets Christians who are living the abundant life, the lack becomes more obvious in his own life. I'll show you how to communicate this without coming across as a religious nut in chapters 15 and 16.

 HIS PERSONALITY TYPE

Consider the personality type of the man you're trying to reach. Some men are the strong, silent type. Others are gregarious. Some are loath to show emotion in public. Many are drawn to achievement.

Fortunately, there are a great variety of entry points to the Christian faith today. With a mixture of prayer and discernment, you can help your man find an entry point that matches his natural bent.

Caroline is a holiness Pentecostal. She's a Spirit-filled Christian who enjoys enthusiastic worship. She works with a man named Karl, who seems open to the gospel. But Karl is the analytical type. She thought about inviting Karl and his family to church, but she senses in her heart that her church is just too wild for Karl. What can she do?

Perhaps Karl might be open to reading an apologetics book, which offers empirical evidence for Christianity. There are many fine apologists today such as Josh McDowell, Lee Strobel, and Ravi Zacharias. Caroline gives one of these books to Karl for Christmas, and soon she's fielding his questions about God.

Janna's husband, Ralph, is the sociable type. He's not much for worship services, but Janna thinks he might be open to attending a church fellowship. Janna asks Ralph's friend, Derek (a member of the church), to invite Ralph to the next fun event. And what do you know? Ralph says yes.

Paula's father, Irv, is an achievement-oriented retired executive. He likes to get things done. He's told Paula he doesn't like going to church because it's a waste of time. So Paula suggests to Irv that he come down and swing a hammer at a Habitat for Humanity project her church is sponsoring. While he's on the job site, he sees Alvin, a former business associate. The two strike up a conversation while pounding nails. Before he knows it, Alvin has invited Irv to his men's group on Thursday morning.

Pablo is a computer geek. He works in the IT department and loves to troubleshoot networking problems. His wife, Gloria, heard that the church needed some computer help, so she mentioned it to her husband. To her surprise, Pablo called the church and offered his assistance. Now he's in the church office once a week to check on the

PCs, rubbing shoulders with Christians there. It's amazing: men who would never sit through a church service are often eager to put their skills to work for God's kingdom.

Every one of these scenarios is based on a true story. The right entry point can make all the difference. The idea is to get him into the orbit of godly men so he can see what a real Christian looks like. There is not a more powerful witness than a man who is fully alive in Christ.

Miracles like this are possible, if you consider a man's personality. When you see a connecting opportunity that dovetails with your man's character and interests, ask God for a chance to make the link. Mention the opportunity, and then pray like crazy that God quickens a desire in your man's heart.

 ## DEALING WITH BOYS

What if your son doesn't want to go to church or Sunday school? Here are some options.

If you are married and your husband is a Christian, talk to him about the situation. If your husband is willing, let him handle your son. The last thing you want is to give your boy the impression that you are the spiritual driver in the family. If your son perceives church as *Mom's thing*, he will bolt. Please—ask your husband to take the lead with this.

If you have no husband or can't get his support, you will have to take matters into your own hands. Pray. Ask God to give you the words the boy needs to hear. If your son is the eldest, remind him he is the man of the house and needs to set an example for the younger ones.

If the young man is in grade school, I think it's within your authority to compel him to go to church. You and your husband should present a united front. "Son, in this family we worship together on Sunday. That's the way it's going to be."

When do you stop making an unwilling boy attend services? The Old Testament age of accountability is thirteen. Past this age I would not force a young man to attend services—especially if you are the one doing the forcing. Of course, you should make every effort to understand his objections. Maybe there is something you can do to help him overcome his dislike or boredom.

Now don't be foolish. Don't promise a young boy, "Just wait until you're thirteen and you won't have to go to church anymore." You've just made rejection of the faith into a rite of passage. You can bet he'll disappear the first Sunday he's a teenager—and he'll feel like a man for doing it.

If your adolescent son chooses to skip services, you don't have to make it cushy. You can tell him he has to stay home (no friends), and that he may not use the TV, computer, or phone, except in an emergency. Why? Be straight with him: Tell him that in your family Sunday morning belongs to God, not friends or the media. Tell him he can use the time to rest, do homework, or worship privately. Sheer boredom may bring him back.

Listen closely. He may not be saying, "I don't want to go to church." He may actually be saying, "I don't want to go to *your* church." In times past, children remained brand-loyal to their parents' denomination. But in our choice-driven culture, today's youngsters often feel the need to strike out on their own spiritual quest.

So be shrewd (Matt. 10:16). Instead of opposing him, say this: "Okay, fine. You're becoming a man. And a man makes his own decisions in spiritual matters. This weekend, choose your own church. Do you have any friends you want to go to church with?" Don't even mention the possibility of him sleeping in. Instead, assume with your tone of voice that he will be going to a church of his choosing.

See what you've done? He is now captain of his own ship. He is no longer riding your Christian coattails; he is responsible for finding his own walk with the Lord.

Here is a reality check: sometimes kids don't want to go to church or youth group because they're at odds with another youngster. They have nothing against God; they're just trying to avoid their human adversary. Do what you can to help reconcile the conflict. But if peace does not come, you might encourage your son to try another youth group. Maybe one of his friends attends a different church. Work with his friend's mother and make the connection.

I know some moms who won't allow their kids to visit another church or youth group. A woman may feel this is being unfaithful to her congregation. Or she's frightened that her kids will be taught weird stuff (or that her kids might like the other church better). Unless your son has been invited to visit an obvious cult or other religion, please don't let your fears stand in the way as he explores the religious landscape.

Freedom to mingle with other Christian youth is especially important if your son grew up in a small church. He's probably come up through nursery and Sunday school with the same handful of kids, so he has no idea how large and diverse the body of Christ truly is. He needs to realize the Good Shepherd has many flocks, not just the little fold he grew up in. These flocks may have a few cute ewes as well. This is how I began going to church again at age fifteen—an appealing young lady invited me.

Remember, your goal is not to worship as a family or to deposit your son's body in the church building. Keep the real prize in mind: a son who is pursuing the Lord on his own. Let God be in control.

⚒ HE'S SO MESSED UP ⚒

Some men are emotional wrecks—and it affects their ability to know and love God. They have been hurt. They are angry. They are addicted.

Their minds are addled by drugs and alcohol. They are so out of touch with their feelings they don't know how to be real. The evil one has booby-trapped their hearts, and they are afraid of untangling the wires or their coping strategies might blow up.

The Christian faith is scary to these men, because they know it means untangling the wires. They will have to be real. Vulnerable. So they remain in emotional captivity because it kind of works for them.

A lot of guys are afraid of God because they've been hurt by a man. That makes it hard for them to trust a masculine deity. A generation of men is growing up with festering father wounds. Simply put, men experience an emotional gash when they fail to receive the love and affirmation of their earthly dad. If a man grew up with an abusive or absent father, he may have a hard time believing he is loved and accepted by his heavenly Father. Psychologist Paul Vitz studied the lives of prominent atheists and found that, in almost every case, they either grew up abandoned or were abused by their fathers.[2]

A wounded man is often afraid to open up, so discipleship becomes difficult. He remains aloof, even among Christian brothers. He may have a hard time trusting God or a male leader for fear he'll be discarded or abused again. He thinks he can never be good enough or work hard enough to earn God's favor. He may be tough on the outside, but inside lives an insecure little boy, unable to move forward emotionally.

If your man suffers from this wound, I'd recommend that you read Gary Smalley and John Trent's book *The Blessing*.[3] This book helped me overcome the legacy of an angry father. If you can get your man to read the book, so much the better. Be sure to praise him any time you see him being a strong, responsible man.

Getting a guy to talk about his father can sometimes neutralize the poison in his heart. Contrast the perfect love of God with the imperfect love of his earthly father. Professional counseling can also help.

$\maltese$

IN MARK 9, Jesus encountered a young man who was completely bound up. He was unable to speak, hurting himself, and terrifying everyone around him. He was suicidal. The disciples had been unable to help the youth, but Jesus knew what to do. He went to war with the demon. With a violent shriek the spirit came out, leaving the young man so drained he appeared to be dead. But Christ took him by the hand and lifted him up, fully restored to health.

Sometime later the disciples asked him, "Why couldn't we drive it out?" Jesus answered, "This kind can come out only by prayer" (vv. 28–29 NIV).

So we've come full circle. This chapter ends as it began: *You cannot save your man. Only God can.* He may have to do some frightening things to restore your man to emotional and spiritual health. Will you let Him do it? And will you pray? Prepare to hit your knees in our next chapter.

YOUR TURN

1. Have you ever pushed a man too hard toward God? If so, when? Tell your sisters about it.

2. Describe your man's emotional state. Is his heart open? Booby-trapped? Can you talk with him about eternal things?

3. Does your man suffer from a father wound? How can you help him?

4. Do you believe it is healthy for adolescents to try other churches and youth groups? Or should they remain faithful to their own congregations?

5. As you read about alternative entry points, did you see one that might work for the man you are praying for? What is your next step in this regard?

TAKE ACTION

Investigate alternative entry points to church for your man.

FOURTEEN

How We Get God off His Holy Duff

I love the film *Shadowlands*. It's the story of C. S. Lewis's unexpected, late-in-life marriage. (Since *Shadowlands* revolves around a romance, it qualifies as a chick flick, but I like it anyway.)

In case you're not familiar with C. S. Lewis, he was an Oxford professor and confirmed atheist whose effort to disprove Christianity resulted in his religious awakening. He went on to become the best-loved Christian writer of the twentieth century, and his books such as *Mere Christianity* and The Chronicles of Narnia series remain best-sellers to this day.

Shadowlands begins in the 1950s, when the never-married Lewis is at the height of his popularity as a writer and speaker. He travels the British Isles, lecturing crowds of women in hats and gloves. One of his adoring fans is a brash American divorcée named Joy Gresham. The two begin corresponding. A friendship sprouts. Lewis eventually agrees to marry her so she can stay in Britain, away from her abusive ex-husband in the States.

Soon after their wedding of convenience, Joy collapses. Cancer has eaten away at her femur. As she lies dying in a hospital bed, Lewis realizes he truly loves her, as she has always loved him. The couple marries again in the hospital, this time before God and family.

Joy is given just weeks to live, but God hears her husband's prayers. Against all odds, her condition improves. When news of this miraculous recovery reaches Oxford, Lewis's friends are joyful. One of them says, "I know how hard you've been praying. God has obviously heard your prayers."

C. S. Lewis offers an astonishing reply. "Prayer doesn't change God. It changes me."

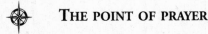

THE POINT OF PRAYER

Prayer does not change God. He has already decided that He wants your man on His team. Prayer changes you. This is why you must persist in prayer—even if it seems like God is taking His time answering. Remember the parable of the persistent widow? In case you've forgotten, I'll recall it here:

> Jesus told his disciples a story about how they should keep on praying and never give up:
>
> In a town there was once a judge who didn't fear God or care about people. In that same town there was a widow who kept going to the judge and saying, "Make sure that I get fair treatment in court." For a while the judge refused to do anything. Finally, he said to himself, "Even though I don't fear God or care about people, I will help this widow because she keeps on bothering me. If I don't help her, she will wear me out."
>
> The Lord said: Think about what that crooked judge said. Won't God protect his chosen ones who pray to him day and night? Won't he be concerned for them? He will surely hurry and help them. But when the Son of Man comes, will he find on this

earth anyone with faith? (Luke 18:1–8 CEV)

The petitioner in this story is a woman. In fact, she is a widow, which would have made her utterly powerless in the first century. You may feel like the widow: powerless to influence your men for Christ. Yet Jesus says that if you persist in prayer, you will receive help.

Look back at Jesus' concluding statement: "But when the Son of Man comes, will he find on this earth anyone with faith?" His question is the key to understanding why we must persist. Christ is looking for faith on this earth. A woman who keeps on praying is putting her faith to the test, strengthening it through the regular exercise of prayer.

Think of how spoiled we would become if God instantly answered our every appeal. We would come to treat God like an ATM—insert prayer, receive answer. We might come to see God's power as emanating from ourselves. Christianity would devolve into a benevolent form of witchcraft, and our prayers would become nothing more than spells.

God's goal is not our happiness. He wants us to depend utterly on Him. This is why answers often do not come right away. But they do come. You may have prayed for years for the men you love but to no avail. Please, don't give up. Prayer doesn't change God—it is changing you.

TAP INTO THE RESOURCE

Anne Scheiber died in 1995 at the age of 101. For years she had lived alone in a cramped apartment. Her furniture was worn bare, and paint was peeling off the walls. In order to save money, she didn't subscribe to the newspaper and rarely ran the air conditioner in order to save money.

She left a $22 million estate.

As children of God, we have at our disposal vast resources in the spiritual realm, but we remain impoverished because we don't draw on our account. We forget to pray. Or we're too busy to pray. Or we don't know how to pray. Or we don't pray in faith, failing to believe God will answer.

> So Jesus answered and said to them, "Have faith in God. For assuredly, I say to you, whoever says to this mountain, 'Be removed and be cast into the sea,' and does not doubt in his heart, but believes that those things he says will be done, he will have whatever he says. Therefore I say to you, whatever things you ask when you pray, believe that you receive them, and you will have them. (Mark 11:22–24)

In this chapter we're going to take a mere glance at the role of prayer in bringing men to God. We are only dipping a toe in deep waters. If you want to dive headlong into prayer, there are many fine books on the subject at your local Christian bookstore.

Here are six ideas that can help.

1. Make It Conversational.

Think about the conversations you have with your friends. Some are short. Others are long and involved. Some are emotionally charged. Others are routine. And so it is with prayer. You are talking to a real person (Jesus) who is alive and wants to hear what you have to say.

Some people think prayer has to be done on the knees, or at certain times of the day, or facing a certain direction, and so on. But Paul commanded us to pray without ceasing (1 Thess. 5:17). That means prayer isn't always something you stop and do; it's an ongoing talk with the Source of life.

Prayer is not a flowery speech; it should sound exactly like a conversation you would have with a friend. Give yourself permission to pray short, spunky prayers. I've found that the more raw and unreligious my prayers sound, the more effective they seem to be. We'll talk more about this in chapter 19, under the topic of *prayer-speak*.

2. Make It Bold.

John Wesley instructed his followers to "storm the throne of grace and persevere therein, and mercy will come down."[1] God loves to answer bold prayers. Just march right in and tell Him what you want.

I think God appreciates prayers that are this bold: "Father, there's this guy at work who is really messing up his life. It ticks me off to see what he's doing to himself and his family. Please get his attention, and use me in whatever way You choose to help him." If your prayers for men are not this bold and plainspoken, kick it up a notch.

3. Fight for Your Men.

Be ready to fight for your men in prayer. Jesus authorized His followers to come against the spiritual forces that bind men's hearts. In Matthew 16:19, Christ said, "Whatever you bind on earth will be bound in heaven, and whatever you loose on earth will be loosed in heaven." Don't be afraid to pray specifically against the spiritual powers that imprison men. You can ask God to take captive specific sins, addictions, and habits that hold your man down. Pray boldly!

This binding and loosing of spirits may seem a little weird to you, especially if you have never hung out with Pentecostals. Evil is real, so don't be afraid to fight the powers of darkness.

One caution I would add: you should never directly address evil spirits or Satan himself when you pray. There is a time for this, but not as a part of your prayer life. Prayer is conversation with God, not Satan. You wouldn't invite the prince of darkness to church; why give him a place in your prayer life? Instead, pray only to God and ask Him to fight for you and your men through His Holy Spirit.

4. Pray the Word.

As you read the Bible, pray the Scriptures back to their Author. When you come across a passage that sums up what you want for your man, speak the Word as your prayer. For example, if you run across this passage: "You will seek me and find me when you seek me with all your heart" (Jer. 29:13 NIV), stop and pray it back to God, asking Him to make it a reality in your man's life.

Let me emphasize that this is not a magic, name-it-and-claim-it formula for bending God to our will. Instead, Scripture is a forge that melts our willfulness and molds our hearts to His revealed truth.

5. Pray with Your Sisters.

Roman soldiers were taught to fight in lines. But if an enemy broke through the ranks and the lines dissolved, they were taught to find two, three, or four of their fellows and fight back-to-back. This tactic allowed the Romans to triumph in battle even when chaos reigned. The saying "I've got your back" is born of this ancient stratagem.

Remember, you are not the only woman who's praying for a man. So get each others' backs. Form a group of two or more women who pray regularly for the men they care about.

If you paid attention in chapter 12, you may already have your circle of sisters. If not, I urge you again to take this step. Jesus specifically told us that wherever two or three are gathered in His name, He will be among them.

6. A *Handy* Reminder to Pray.

How do you remember to pray for your men persistently? Here's an idea: Look down at your hand. How many fingers do you see? (Don't be a smart aleck; count your thumb too.)

Choose five men who need closer fellowship with Christ. Assign one finger to each man. Then, every time you're waiting in line, driving in the car, or sitting on an airplane, touch one finger at a time and pray for the corresponding man. This is a quick, easy-to-remember way to keep your men constantly before the Father.

※

I CHOSE THE title of this chapter to get your attention, but it's theologically incorrect. Prayer does not get God off His holy duff. He is already at work. Prayer aligns you with His Spirit so you can better participate in the work He is already doing in your man's heart. C. S. Lewis was right: prayer does not change God; it changes you.

As I write this, I'm sitting by a creek swollen with spring runoff. Planted next to the creek is a willow. For six months it's resembled nothing more than a collection of dead twigs planted in frozen, lifeless soil. But now green buds are popping out on every branch. In a few days the willow will burst into full leaf.

Your men may seem spiritually dead, cold, and frozen. But like the willow, spring will come. Life will return. Don't ever give up praying for the men you love.

YOUR TURN

1. Do you have your circle of sisters yet? I'm going to keep hounding you until you do.

2. Are you persistent in prayer, or do you give up easily?

3. Are your prayers bold or timid? Do you storm the throne of grace, or do you approach God on tiptoe?

4. Is it easier to pray alone or in a group?

5. Have you ever prayed the Scriptures back to God? How did it affect your prayers?

TAKE ACTION

Pray with another woman this week—in person, if you can. If not, you can pray with her over the phone.

FIFTEEN

Your Words Whisper; Your Life Shouts

Apparently this problem of missing men is nothing new. Way back in AD 70, the apostle Peter noticed a number of Christian wives attending the 11:00 a.m. service without their husbands. So Mr. Keys-to-the-Kingdom offered the following advice. I've quoted it from the New American Standard Bible, one of the most literal English translations. Read it slowly and carefully:

> In the same way, you wives, be submissive to your own husbands so that even if any of them are disobedient to the word, they may be won without a word by the behavior of their wives, as they observe your chaste and respectful behavior.
>
> Your adornment must not be merely external—braiding the hair, and wearing gold jewelry, or putting on dresses; but let it be the hidden person of the heart, with the imperishable quality of a gentle and quiet spirit, which is precious in the sight of God.
>
> For in this way in former times the holy women also, who hoped in God, used to adorn themselves, being submissive to their own husbands; just as Sarah obeyed Abraham, calling him lord,

and you have become her children if you do what is right without being frightened by any fear. (1 Pet. 3:1–6 NASB)

The amazing promise of this passage comes in the first sentence: "they may be won without a word." Does this mean you can share your faith without saying anything? Without explaining the four spiritual laws? Without leaving tracts in the bathroom? That's right. Peter's witnessing advice boils down to two words: *zip it.*

As Saint Francis said, "Preach the gospel. If necessary, use words." A verbal witness should be your last resort, only when your man requests it. In the meantime, your life is the tract he'll be reading.

In chapter 13 I told you the pressure is off—only God can change the heart of a man. Now the apostle Peter seems to be putting the pressure back on. It's up to you again—or is it? What's a girl to do?

SIX WAYS TO WHET HIS APPETITE FOR GOD

Let's break down Peter's strategy. As I read the passage, I see six action points: *be submissive, be chaste, be respectful, cultivate a gentle and quiet spirit, do what is right,* and *do not be afraid.* None of these alone will win a man to Christ. But a woman who exhibits these six characteristics will create a hunger for God in the hearts of the men who know her. Let's take a closer look at each of these.

1. Be Submissive.

Right out of the starting gate, Peter uses the hot-button term *submissive.* In fact, he pushes the button twice for good measure.

The word *submissive* sounds so backward in our day of feminism and gender equality. What does this emotionally charged word really mean?

You know that thing on your porch that you wipe your feet on before coming in the house? It says WELCOME on it? Being submissive does not make you one of these. Your husband is not supposed to make all the decisions while you sit by passively, doing the dishes and straightening your pearls. Nor does this passage give him license to carouse and cheat while you put on a happy face. Some women take submission to the extreme, quietly enduring the abuse of their children or themselves in hope of a heavenly rescue. (Please note that this passage is written to wives regarding their husbands. This scripture does not instruct women to submit to any other man.)

Submission is not blind obedience. True submission comes when a woman *voluntarily* relinquishes her power in order to build up her man. She puts his needs ahead of her own. She finds ways to please him. She makes him feel loved and needed. She supports him instead of second-guessing or criticizing. She treats him as a partner to be loved, not a problem to be fixed.

Sometimes women have a hard time submitting, even when their husbands are reasonable. Once again, it goes back to the curse. Women have an inborn need to control (Gen. 3). They often feel they know better than their husbands—especially when it comes to relationships. But if wives would voluntarily relinquish that control, God would work through their husbands—even husbands who do not yet know Him.

Can submission go too far? What if your husband wants you to sin? Anita questioned, "What if he tells me I can't go to church, or I can't donate any money to my congregation?" Carmen asked, "My husband wants me to do things that are illegal. Do I submit?"

The answer is a big, red *no*. You submit to God first and your husband second. For example, the Bible says we are not to forsake meeting together (Heb. 10:25). So if your husband tells you to stop going to church, go anyway. The Scriptures command you to give, so you should continue giving.

Now, be reasonable. If you're going to church three or four times a week, cut back to once or join a women's study group that meets at a time your husband won't miss you. And if you want to put something in the offering plate, give only money you have earned yourself. Also, the Scriptures tell us to submit to earthly governments (Rom. 13:1), so you must not engage in illegal activities, even if your husband commands you to do so.

Now what about submission in the bedroom? It may be hard to work up any romantic enthusiasm if you and hubby are living in different spiritual zip codes. If he is mean or critical, it may be very hard to have sex with him—let alone enjoy it.

I'm no Dr. Phil, but Dr. Paul told us, "Husbands and wives should be fair with each other about having sex. A wife belongs to her husband instead of to herself, and a husband belongs to his wife instead of to himself. So don't refuse sex to each other" (1 Cor. 7:3–5 CEV).

I'm delighted to report that a lot of Christian wives have taken this verse to heart. A study from the University of Chicago found that conservative, Protestant women enjoy the best sex lives, followed by mainline Protestants and Catholics. And those swinging secular women? They finished last.[1]

Wives, you will not win your husband to Christ in bed, but you can drive him away from church if you freeze him out. Remember, God is the source of all love. Ask the Lord for a forgiving heart and a supernatural passion for your husband.

2. Be Chaste.

Whew. We're through submission. What's Peter's next nugget of wisdom? He says that men can be won *as they observe your chaste . . . behavior.*

Chaste is an old-fashioned word that means pure. Men respond to the gospel when they see you living a life of purity. Here's an illustration to help you understand what purity is—and what it is not.

Sometimes the Murrow family invites guests over, but the house isn't completely tidy. Minutes before company arrives, we'll gather the mess, throw it in the laundry room, and bar the door so our visitors don't see it.

A chaste life is not necessarily a perfectly clean spiritual house. You might still have some messes. But a life of purity means there are no secret rooms that are inaccessible to the Holy Spirit. Jesus is free to open every door and deal with every mess.

Purity is not perfection; it is complete openness to God. When reaching out to men, you should avoid uptight perfectionism. A prim, proper Mary Poppins–type spiritual life (practically perfect in every way!) will drive your men away from the Lord. Your perfectionism makes men feel judged, especially if you subtly impose your standards on them. For example, if the Spirit convicts you to give up alcohol, don't harangue your father about his glass of wine with dinner. Let the Lord speak to him.

3. Be Respectful.

Peter also exhorts women to be *respectful*. Don't undermine your husband in front of the kids. Try not to second-guess his decisions. Don't argue over the small things, even if you disagree. Hold him in high esteem to his face—and behind his back. Lose a fight now and then.

Another way to show respect to your husband is to get interested in what he likes. Let's say he's a classic car buff, but you don't know a carburetor from a crankshaft. Don't pout when he's out working on his machine; go out and see what he's up to. Take him some refreshments. If he likes company, pick up a rag and start polishing chrome. That's respect. Get into his world, and he'll be more likely to ask about yours.

4. Cultivate a Gentle and Quiet Spirit.

Now, on to the subject of beauty. Read the passage closely. Dressing up and looking nice is not a sin. Instead, Peter cautions women not to focus solely on their outward appearance. The apostle reminds us that true beauty springs from a gentle and quiet spirit (1 Pet. 3:4).

This passage has been misinterpreted over the centuries. In the past, Christian women have taken it to mean they must be mousy, timid, or plain. This is precisely the opposite of what you want to do. Let me share a beauty secret you'll never read in a checkout stand magazine: *if you want to be attractive, be confident.* Your dress size doesn't matter: men are drawn to women who are self-assured, relaxed, and enjoying life. On the flip side, a supermodel who is stressed, neurotic, or demanding will drive men off. Ever wondered why the world's most beautiful women can't seem to find lasting relationships?

A woman with a quiet, confident spirit will attract men. This is true beauty. It makes you—and your faith—irresistible to the opposite sex.

Take a moment to read the fruit of the Spirit passage in Galatians 5:22–23. If you do not have more love, more joy, more peace, and more patience than your man, he will see no reason to follow Christ. Bill Hybels put it this way: "As your [man] is watching your life, he is doing a quiet evaluation, asking himself whether he would be a winner or a loser if he, too, began to follow Jesus. He is wondering, *Would Christianity be an upgrade over my current situation?*"[2]

Lee Strobel continues the thought: "Are you living the kind of Christian life your [man] would see as a trade up? If your Christian life is strangled by legalism, parched by gloom, pinched by a desire to control, smothered by somberness, or numbed by boredom, nobody in his right mind would want that kind of life for himself."[3]

Let me put this into masculine terms. You are competing for your man's heart; therefore you have to beat him at the game of life. Your life has to be so much better than his that it's a slam-dunk. Even when trials come. Even if the man you're praying for is putting you through these trials.

Men can be cruel. Sometimes the men you know best become your worst persecutors. Jesus predicted this (Matt. 10:34–36). A man you care about may make fun of your faith, call you names, or lambaste your Christian friends. Do not be surprised: "All who desire to live godly in Christ Jesus will suffer persecution" (2 Tim. 3:12).

Why would a man you care about be so mean? Maybe he's trying to see if your faith is real. Pressure is a guy's way of testing your resolve. So if you defend yourself with a respectful tone, he might think more of you than if you just sit back and take the abuse. Tell him, "Look, my faith in God is very important to me. I'd appreciate it if you'd show me a little more respect." Men admire people who stand up for themselves and don't back down.

In the meantime, follow the teaching of Jesus: *pray for those who persecute you* (Matt. 5:44). The shots you're taking are nothing compared to the blows persecuted Christians endure in places like North Korea. Don't retaliate, browbeat him, or shoot him the icy stare of a self-righteous woman. Resist the urge to mutter, "God will get you for that!"

Another way you can exhibit a quiet and gentle spirit is to go easy on the Christian subculture. Nancy Kennedy, in her book *When He Doesn't Believe,* quotes a man named Rick whose wife went loopy for the Lord: "If she's not blasting the religious music, she's got the religious TV programs going," he said. "She's always reading to me out of the Bible, trying to get me to listen. I can't take it! If I wanted to believe and go to church before, I don't want to now."[4]

On the other hand, Leslie Strobel scored points with her then-atheist husband by putting away her Bible and greeting him warmly whenever he came into the room. She wasn't hiding her faith. She was simply communicating to her husband that he was more important than her religious routines.

5. Do What Is Right.

Peter concluded his instructions with a call to "do what is right" (1 Pet. 3:6 NASB). Let me suggest a couple of ways you can *do right* by your men.

Back in chapter 3, I briefly mentioned how men sometimes

become jealous of the church. In trying to put God first, some women end up putting their church first. This breeds resentment. If you're always out ministering to others but not to your family, the men of your household will come to despise your religion.

I lived this nightmare for years. My wife, Gina, is a preacher's kid. From an early age, she was programmed to drop everything if someone had a need. She would disappear for hours, doing the Lord's work. I was left to care for two small children, who kept asking, "Where is Mommy?" (This was back in the days before cell phones.) Even though I was a disciple of Jesus, I began to begrudge the church, since it got so much of my wife's time and attention.

I would also call your attention to a dangerous fad sweeping church today: women imagining themselves married to Jesus. It's hard to pick up a Christian book for women these days without finding language such as this: *I saw Him as a lover, a Bridegroom, eager to satisfy the object of His desire—me! I faced the One who had been courting me . . . I received a marriage proposal from the One who loved me . . . We would be together forever, we'd laugh together, we'd love each other.*[5]

Today's Christian music piles on more romantic imagery. According to these tunes, Christ's disciples should be desperate for Him, long for His embrace, and become caught up in the wonder of His touch. They should rest in His arms and experience His kiss of love. Many songs encourage believers to fall in love with Jesus.

These new interpretations spring from a misunderstanding of the biblical term *bride of Christ*. Authors and musicians are encouraging women to think of themselves as brides, married to Christ Himself. But what does the Bible say? There is only one bride of Christ: the church (all followers of Jesus throughout history). Jesus is already engaged, and He has no interest in a tryst with you.

There is a very good reason Christian authors and composers insert this romantic imagery—it sells. Women buy up to 75 percent of Christian products. Many of these women are single or trapped in loveless marriages. So a passionate Jesus opens their hearts—and their wallets. It's just savvy marketing.

If you are entertaining a fantasy of Christ as lover, stop it. Not only is husband-Jesus unbiblical, your reverie may poison your love for your earthly husband or boyfriend. How is he supposed to measure up to Christ? Fantasy Jesus is the perfect lover who never raises His voice, never works too much, and never has gas. Your man of flesh will always fall short, and you'll find yourself increasingly disappointed and critical of him.

6. Do Not Be Afraid.

Peter concludes his advice with this little phrase: "without being frightened by any fear" (1 Pet. 3:6 NASB). A fearless woman is irresistibly attractive to men.

But here is a painful truth: many Christian women are bound up in fear. Fear for their children. Fear of worldly influences. Fear of change. In fact, many women go to church not because they want to courageously follow Jesus, but because religion promises to bring safety and order to their chaotic lives.

Women, if you use the church as a security blanket, don't expect men to follow you into the pew. If you treat the church as your root system and Christ as your divine bodyguard—forget it. The masculine imagination is fired by adventure, challenge, and danger. It is only as men see you taking risks for God's kingdom that your life will become a draw.

How can you loosen your grip on the security blanket? Take stock of your Christian life. Many women focus their spiritual lives on *learning about God.* They take classes. They attend seminars. They go to Bible studies. Their spiritual life becomes a series of book-on-the-lap experiences. If they serve, they do so in safe, predictable venues such as classrooms, choirs, nurseries, and kitchens.

But when your focus shifts from *learning about God* to *having adventures with God,* men take notice. When a man sees a woman taking risks and changing the world, it becomes very hard for him to criticize her faith. My wife, Gina, will have something to say about this in chapter 17.

If you are not taking risks that a man would be impressed with, you may need to make a change. Does this frighten you? Good. Get on your knees and ask God what big, frightening thing He would have you do.

YOUR TURN

1. Be honest: what percentage of your Christian life consists of reading books, singing, and listening to pastors/teachers?

2. Do you go to church for comfort or for adventure?

3. What do you think submission means? Is it hard to do?

4. What is one way you can outlive the man you care about?

5. When should you quietly endure persecution for your faith? When should you stand up for yourself?

TAKE ACTION

This week, do something frightening for God.

SIXTEEN

How to Talk to Men About God

So ladies, how are we doing? That last couple of chapters were a wee bit challenging, no? Submission . . . risk taking . . . persecution. The very idea of sharing your faith without words is probably stressing you out.

Women often try to talk their men into the kingdom. It's so logical; after all, the Bible says, "Faith comes by hearing" (Rom. 10:17). Women think, *he needs to know the truth of God's Word. So I'll pray, and then I'll tell him about Jesus.*

As we've seen, a verbal witness is often the worst way to reach a guy. But when a woman lets her life do the talking, men get curious. Linda Davis wrote:

> [He] may be expecting to be badgered about going to church or reading the Bible. When you don't say a word about these things, he will at first be greatly relieved. Then, as he sees you growing in peace and joy, he may become curious. But don't speak up yet. The cardinal rule of bargaining is, "The first one to make an offer loses." It's a waiting game. Let him stew until he can stand the quiet no more and comes to you with his questions or offers to go to church.[1]

IT'S GOOD TO be quiet about your faith. But sometimes, out of the blue, your man pops the question. He wants to talk about God.

Here's an illustration. One evening, Linda is standing in the kitchen chopping vegetables. Her sixteen-year-old son, Eric, who's had no interest in Christ for years, is preparing to set the table. Out of the blue Eric says, "Mom, I saw this movie with Orlando Bloom. It was about the Crusades. Anyway, Orlando Bloom's wife committed suicide, and the priest said she wouldn't go to heaven. Was he right?"

Linda turns to her beloved son. She looks deeply into his eyes. She says, "Son, I'm so glad you asked that question." Then Linda launches into a ten-thousand-word explanation of the doctrine of atonement, concluding that Christ died on the cross as a propitiation for our sins, and if we'll only receive Him, we will enjoy eternity in heaven. All the while, she's holding a knife.

How do you think Eric would respond? Honestly, if you handle a man's spiritual question the way Linda did, he will never ask you another one.

You need to be ready for that unexpected moment when a man pokes his nose under the tent of faith. In this chapter we'll examine how to react, what to say, and, most importantly, what *not* to say when that moment comes.

 REMAIN CALM

It is absolutely essential that you do not overreact to his interest in Christ. Resist the urge to cry, hug, or even smile broadly at him. Don't treat his inquiry any differently than any other question he might ask. You may feel like a cheerleader on the inside, but you're a Secret Service agent on the outside.

Linda should have kept on chopping vegetables. No turning to her son. No looking him in the eyes. When a woman plays it cool, she puts her man at ease.

⌐ LET HIM DO THE TALKING ⌐

In evangelism training, you're taught how to talk about your faith. Well, guess what? When witnessing to a man, you want *him* to do the talking. Does this seem strange? Look at how Jesus witnessed. He rarely gave people the answers. Instead, He asked men great questions or told mysterious stories. Then He let them discover answers for themselves.

Let's go back to the kitchen and see how Linda might have used questions to get her son talking. We pick up the dialogue midstream:

ERIC: Anyway, Orlando Bloom's wife committed suicide, and the priest said she wouldn't go to heaven. Was he right?

LINDA: Well, what do you think?

ERIC: I don't know.

LINDA: How do you think God determines who goes to heaven and who doesn't?

(If Eric grew up in an evangelical church and paid attention, his next response should be something like the following:)

ERIC: The people who believe in Jesus go to heaven.

LINDA: I agree with you. Why are you curious about suicide?

ERIC: There's this guy at school who committed suicide last month. I was just wondering if he went to heaven or not.

Aha. By asking questions, Linda has figured out what's really on her son's heart.

You don't want to be the Bible Answer Woman. Answers shut a

man down, but questions open him up. The more he talks, the more comfortable he'll be with the conversation. A lot of guys have wondered about spiritual things but have never talked about them. If a man learns that he can bring you his questions without getting a gospel sales pitch, he'll learn to trust you. And as you listen, you'll learn what's really going on inside his head.

Now, maybe the conversation goes like this:

ERIC: Who gets into heaven? I don't know. Maybe the people who do good things with their lives, like Mother Teresa or something.

LINDA: Do you know what the Bible says about this?

ERIC: No.

LINDA: Would you like to know?

If Eric says yes, then Linda can share the gospel with her son's permission. If he says no, the door is still open to future conversations because she didn't try to steamroll him.

 ## PUT DOWN YOUR RED PENCIL

In the midst of a spiritual conversation, a man may say something that's theologically questionable or just plain wrong. A woman's tendency is to correct the error. You just want to help—but this is a strategic mistake. If you correct a man, you'll stop the conversation in its tracks. Observe:

ERIC: Who gets into heaven? I don't know. Maybe the people who do good things with their lives, like Mother Teresa or something.

LINDA: No, God's Word says that it is by grace you are saved, through faith. It's not the people who do good works who go to heaven; it's the people who trust in Christ to forgive their sins who spend eternity with Him.

ERIC: (no response)

Linda's mistake was leaving Eric with nothing to say. What is he supposed to do, short of falling on his knees and repenting of his sins? She also ran the risk of making him feel dumb, reinforcing the common male notion that women are spiritually superior.

It is very important not to give a man an answer unless he asks for it. The goal is not to red-pencil his theology; you want him seeking God for himself. When you spoon-feed a man Bible answers, you short-circuit his discovery process.

Sometimes guys will come up with the most off-the-wall questions. "If God is all-powerful, then why is there suffering in the world?" "Why doesn't everyone go to heaven?" "Aren't all religions the same?" Answer these questions with questions if you can. Let the man talk himself into a corner. Allow him to hear the absurdity of his beliefs from his own mouth. By all means, avoid a heated argument. Be confident, but stay cool.

 ## BLAME IT ON GOD

Eventually a man may ask for a straight answer. You may have to say something that offends him, such as, "I do believe that Jesus is the only way to heaven." If he accuses you of being narrow-minded, blame it on God. "Hey, this isn't my opinion. Jesus said: 'No man comes to the Father but by Me.' If you have a problem with that, then take it up with Jesus."

If you don't have an answer for a man's question, say so. He will appreciate your humility. Offer to search for the answer with him, or suggests some ways he can find it himself.

Break the Ice

Once in a while, it makes sense to initiate a spiritual conversation with a man. Let's say you're feeling the prompting of God to share your faith with a male coworker. The subject has never come up in conversation. Rumors are swirling that he may be transferred to another city, so it's now or never. What do you do?

A good icebreaker is to ask him about his religious background. Try an opening question such as, "Tell me, Stu, did you grow up in a religious home like I did?" Or "Hey, Manny, I'm curious. Were you a church kid like me?" These starters invite men to share an aspect of religion they know well—their own experience. Listen carefully and look for points of common background. "You had a Sunday school teacher with cat-eye glasses? So did I!"

Once a man seems comfortable talking about faith matters, you may have an opportunity to invite him to church or initiate another spiritual conversation later. Who knows what God might do?

There are other ways to start the conversation. If there's a religion story in the news, ask your man what he thinks of it. If a local church makes the news, get his take on it. The idea is to get him used to talking about God stuff with you and to reassure him you're not the door-to-door Jesus saleslady.

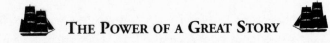 **The Power of a Great Story**

One of the best ways to share the good news with men is through stories. This was Jesus' MO. If you add an object or some visual component to your story, so much the better.

A personal story or testimony is particularly powerful. If you have an account of God's work in your life, don't be afraid to share it. Men don't like to be preached at, but a personal story slips right past their defenses.

For example, Linda had an uncle who committed suicide when she was young. Now might be the perfect moment to share that story with her son and tell how the tragedy eventually led her cousin to faith in Christ.

⌐ Metaphors Matter ¬

By now you probably know that the metaphors you use make a difference. Don't say to your man, "Ralph, Jesus is in love with you. He's pursuing you for a passionate, intimate relationship." If this metaphor *does* appeal to your man, he may need counseling.

In fact, it might be helpful to jettison the *personal relationship with Jesus* lingo altogether when sharing your faith with men. Instead, talk about the freedom you experience when you walk closely with God. Communicate the adventure of following Jesus. Speak of the cause of Christ and the sacrifices men are making for it. This language seems odd today, but it's actually truer to the biblical narrative.

If You Died Tonight . . .

Did you know young men are immortal? That's why the traditional heaven-focused approach to evangelism doesn't work well with adolescent males. The usual set-up question—"If you died tonight, do you know where you would spend eternity?"—doesn't wash with guys under twenty-five, because they believe they are never going to die.

Today's evangelism training is much more comprehensive. I'd encourage you to take a course in sharing your faith. There are also many good books on lifestyle evangelism, which teach you how to bring up spiritual matters in the regular course of life.

BLESSED BREVITY

First Peter 3:15 says we should always be ready to give an answer for the hope we have—but that answer doesn't have to be long and drawn out.

Brevity is bliss to men. The male brain just can't process a torrent of words. Jesus knew this. As I pointed out in chapter 9, the average parable of Jesus preaches in just thirty-eight seconds. Christ reduced the Law and the Prophets to two sentences. He gave us the entire gospel in a single verse: John 3:16.

Some women have a very hard time being succinct. They're used to talking with their girlfriends, discussing issues at length from every possible angle. So when they talk about something as important as faith, they suffer diarrhea of the mouth (a crude but accurate description of how men feel when women spew words at them).

Men like to get to the point. So be concise. Why use one hundred words when a dozen will do?

Jesus kept His lessons brief so His disciples would be left wanting more. Please, don't pre-chew the gospel for your man—challenge him to get into the Word and find answers himself. Your goal is not to give him truth. You want your man to discover the Way, the Truth, and the Life for himself.

YOUR TURN

1. When you have something to say, do you talk a little or a lot?

2. Do you like to talk about your faith? Why or why not?

3. Are you good at asking questions, or do you prefer to give people answers?

4. Have you ever shared your faith with a man? Tell the group about it.

5. If you're not going to describe discipleship as a personal relationship with Jesus, how will you describe it?

TAKE ACTION

Role-play a spiritual conversation with another woman. Take turns playing the role of a man who does not know Christ. Practice asking questions and being concise.

How to Lead Boys to Faith

I just read that John Stott announced his retirement from the ministry at the age of eighty-six. Stott is an Anglican priest, a world-renowned theologian, and a strong voice for evangelicalism in the Church of England. He is the author of many books and Bible commentaries. Billy Graham once called Stott "the most respected clergyman in the world today."[1]

Who introduced this lion of the faith to Jesus? His mother. Stott's father was an agnostic and avowed scientific secularist, but his mother took the boy to church, encouraged him to read his Bible, and taught him to say his prayers. Although Stott's faith did not blossom until he was seventeen, his mother's persistent witness planted the seed and tilled the soil of his heart.

There are many others. Abraham Lincoln was strongly influenced by his mother's religious convictions. Super Bowl coach Lovie Smith, one of the NFL's most outspoken believers, was taken to church by his mother, while his alcoholic father stayed away. The apostle Paul traced Timothy's spiritual lineage through his grandmother and his mother (2 Tim. 1:5).

So it does happen. Women do lead young men to Christ. But it's a long shot.

It's all about Dad

Researchers from Switzerland examined whether parents' religious habits were transmitted to their offspring. They studied different variables, but one critical factor towered above the rest: the practices of the father determine whether children grow up attending church. And here's the shocker: Mom's religiosity has almost no influence over her kids' future devotion.

Consider these findings:

- When Mom is a regular churchgoer but Dad attends infrequently (or never), just 2 to 3 percent of their kids go on to become regular churchgoers.
- When both Mom and Dad attend church regularly, 33 percent of kids grow up as regular attendees.
- Here's the real bombshell: when Dad is faithful but Mom never attends, 44 percent of the kids end up as regular churchgoers. This is the highest outcome of any scenario.[2]

This study seems to indicate that in spiritual matters, kids take their cues from Dad—at least in Switzerland. But does the pattern hold in the United States?

LifeWay research surveyed more than one thousand adults age eighteen to thirty who had attended a Protestant church in high school. The study found that 70 percent of these "raised in church" kids stopped attending for at least a year between the ages of eighteen and twenty-two. Researchers studied what caused them to drop out and what factors kept them faithful. And what do you know: those kids whose fathers attended church regularly were much less likely to disappear as young adults. The researchers wrote, "While more mothers attend church, the father's attendance makes a bigger impact on the decision to stay in church."[3]

 ## FAITH PASSES MAN TO MAN

Ready for some more bad news? Researchers Paul Hill, David Anderson, and Roland Martinson interviewed eighty-eight young men to identify the key relationships through which faith is imparted. Here's what they found:

Relationship That Influenced Men's Faith	Number of Men Who Mentioned This
Family of origin	42
Male mentors	32
Friends	24
Marriage (out of 29 married men)	23
Fathers	21
Extended family	19
Acquaintances	14
Mothers	11

Note how often the Christian faith passes from man to man. Male mentors, friends, and fathers appear high on the list. However, only eleven of the eighty-eight men mentioned their mothers as an influence in their faith journey.[4] (On a positive note, twenty-three of twenty-nine married men mentioned their wives.)

Think about the families with children in your church. When the father is actively involved, aren't his children usually involved as well? Now think about those Sunday morning widows, trying to raise faithful children without Dad's help. How devout are her teenagers?

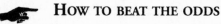 ## How to beat the odds

Mothers, have your mouths gone dry? It's time you faced the truth: it's nigh unto impossible for women to transmit the Christian faith to boys. Lucky for you, our God specializes in the impossible.

I happen to be typing this paragraph on the first Saturday in May. In a few hours twenty horses will compete in the most exciting two minutes in sports, the Kentucky Derby. A few years ago, a lightly regarded stallion named Giacomo entered the race a fifty-to-one shot, but he finished the day under a blanket of roses.

I'll say it again: as a woman, you face long odds in trying to lead your young man to Christ. If you believe the study from Switzerland, it's fifty-to-one. But don't despair. There are things you can do to improve your odds. Most of the suggestions in this chapter are designed to help you get out of the Holy Spirit's way so He can call your young man to follow Him. Who knows? Maybe you'll raise the next John Stott.

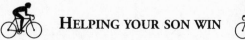 ## Helping your son win

Let's start with the little boys.

The best thing you can do for your tiger cub is consistently implant the idea that church is a guy thing. You want him to see that men are just as involved in the church as women—or even more so. Here's a game plan:

- If your husband goes to church, ask him to get the boy up for church on Sunday morning. He should walk your son to his Sunday school class. Instead of just dropping the boy off, your husband should walk into the class and greet the teacher (who hopefully is a man).
- Ask your husband to lead prayers at mealtime and/or bedtime. If he's willing to read a short devotional, so much the better.
- If your husband is involved in any other spiritual pursuits, let it be known to your son. Encourage your husband to mention these activities often. Meanwhile, keep the spotlight off your Christian activities.
- Ask hubby to show some enthusiasm about church. He should keep his criticisms to himself. Little boys do what they see Daddy doing.
- If you have no husband or your husband is not a believer, this role can go to the eldest brother if he is willing.
- If you attend a church where women do most of the work while men sit passively by, your boy doesn't stand a chance. It might be time to look for a different congregation.

A SUNDAY SCHOOL THAT BOYS WILL LOVE

You and your sisters can revolutionize your Sunday school. Gather your gals and take the Sunday school superintendent or education minister out to lunch. Suggest to her that separating boys and girls would help retain the males as they grow up. Even a small church would be wise to offer boy-only and girl-only classes—even if it's necessary to combine grades. Gender identification is more important than age grouping.

Offer to help her select a curriculum that's boy-friendly. Share some of the ideas you learned in chapter 6 of this book. Tell her you'll support her if a few old-timers object that the kids aren't miserable enough in Sunday school—like they were back in the good old days.

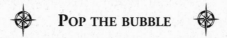

POP THE BUBBLE

Two chapters ago, I cautioned you about using Christianity as a security blanket. Building on that theme, I want to warn you about the *Christian bubble*—the safety-oriented subculture women build around themselves and their loved ones. Mothers are particularly good at blowing these bubbles, because it creates the illusion that their children are protected.

My wife, Gina, is the cofounder of the Fearless Women's Weekend, a Christian ministry that helps women pop their Christian bubbles. "Our churches are full of women who see the church as a defensive force," Gina says. "They put their kids in Christian schools for protection. They listen to family-safe Christian radio in the car. They send their kids to youth group so they won't take drugs or have sex. Women see their main job as keeping their families safe, and the church serves as a bodyguard for their kids."

I must tread lightly here. There is nothing wrong with shielding your family from negative influences. Christian schools, music, and youth group can be a great choice for some. But if Christianity comes across as a safety program, your boys will run from it. Why? Young men despise anything that is safe. Adolescents want to be known as adventurous, risky, and dangerous. C'mon, what sixteen-year-old boy is going to listen to a radio station that bills itself as "safe for the whole family"?

How do you pierce your bubble without exposing your family to harmful influences? Here are a few ideas:

- Stop praying for safety. I challenge you to go thirty days without asking God to protect your kids. Instead, ask Him to do whatever He wants with your children. That's real faith.
- Never refer to Christianity as something that keeps people safe. You'll make it sound like a bicycle helmet.
- Listen to a secular radio station in the car once in a while. It doesn't have to be vulgar, just something besides prerecorded sermons and "Jesus is my boyfriend" music.
- Try not to be too afraid of pop culture. If you're panicked by Pokémon and Harry Potter, your boys will think Christianity is for scaredy-cats.
- Tell your boys the stories of martyrs. Let them know that even today men are making great sacrifices and dying horrible deaths for the cause of Christ.
- Let me say this again: you must take some risks for God. If your faith consists mainly of meetings, study, and contemplation, then add in some action.

How do you deal with popular culture and its corrupting influence? Here's my advice: confront the culture rather than trying to completely shield your kids from it. Unless you live on a deserted island with no TV, Internet, cell phones, or magazines, you'll probably fail anyway.

I tell you the truth: your kids are being bombarded with unholy things, so rejoice! You want this to happen while they are under your roof so you have the opportunity to explain right from wrong. The worst scenario has them growing up naive and then discovering the pleasures of the flesh on the cusp of adulthood. Paul Coughlin wrote, "I believe that in our well-intentioned attempts to protect our children from sin, we're keeping them from life. . . . I've seen what 'sweet Christian girls' do in college after escaping their overprotective homes; their parents would tear their clothing and sit in ashes if they only knew."[5]

Of course, you needn't open the floodgates to all the sewage our culture has to offer. It's perfectly right to monitor your family's Internet usage and limit their TV. The Murrow family finally pulled the plug on cable TV a couple of years ago. Even on the family channels, some of the commercials bordered on the obscene. I made sure the kids knew this was my decision, not their mother's.

I guess the bottom line is this: don't be scared of culture; instead, use it as a tool to teach your kids right from wrong. Fight back. Your sons will admire you if you do this, but they will resist having a bubble blown around them.

Movies are a constant battleground. If I'm watching a movie with my family at home and a morally questionable scene pops up, I usually skip past it with the remote (I love DVDs). I stop and explain to the kids why I refuse to show those images in my house. I often make fun of the filmmakers, pointing out how love doesn't work this way in real life or how violence of that sort would not solve the hero's problems. Call sin what it is—folly. You don't have to preach a sermon until your kids beg, "Mom, can we get back to the movie?" But when evil shows up in your living room, don't be afraid to take it captive. Christianity is meant to engage the culture, not retreat from it.

HAND ME THE RUDDER

You cannot force a boy to be a Christian. In an earlier chapter, I suggested by age thirteen the decision to attend church should be his. But what about everything else, such as youth group, Sunday school, Bible studies, and the like? Same policy. Once a boy reaches his teens, he should be steering his own spiritual ship. If your teenage son starts to rebel, give him the rudder and place him in God's hands.

Still, you can do a little behind-the-scenes orchestrating, as long as you keep it on the QT. If your church has a youth retreat coming up, see if one of his buddies will make the invitation. Some churches take their kids on youth mission trips to places like Mexico. Ask your son's Spanish teacher to suggest that he go and practice his language skills.

Another thing you can do is ask your youth leader what the group is doing for its boys. As meetings and events are planned, is any effort being made to specifically attract and retain guys? Is the singing short and fun? Are the lessons visual and interactive? Do the kids get to move around? Is there question-and-answer time? Don't take a prosecutorial tone with the youth leader; let him or her know that you are concerned for your son and that you want to help.

If your church's youth group is a poor fit for your son, try Young Life, an organization dedicated to reaching kids who weren't raised in church. Its methods are especially effective with boys. Young Life meetings are very active, the messages and songs are brief, and there is an intentional effort to place boys with male mentors.

A generation ago, Larry Norman, the father of Christian rock, asked, "Why should the devil have all the good music?" Happily, this is no longer the case. There's Christian music out there you'd probably hate but your son might love. Big youth gatherings such as BattleCry, Christian music festivals, and conferences can also help. Be careful about pushing these things too hard (slipping a CD into his backpack might be a little much), but if your son has a friend who's into these things, that's a friendship you want to foster.

⚒ THE RIGHT BIBLE ⚒

How do you get a boy to read his Bible? Don't give him one. A woman should never give a Bible to a boy. It should be bestowed upon him by a man he respects. And the cover should not have pictures of children on it. Choose a Bible that looks manly—even for little boys. I recently saw a Bible covered in military camouflage. That's the idea.

If he expresses a desire for a Bible, suggest he earn the money and buy it himself. If he sinks his own cash into a Bible, he's more likely to read it. If this doesn't work, you can still purchase one behind the scenes, but have a man do the giving.

It's important to choose a modern translation. Remember, boys aren't the most fluent readers, and if God's Word is written in the language of Shakespeare, he'll read two or three pages and decide the Bible is not for him.

When I was in seventh grade, I got a bad case of chicken pox, which kept me out of school for two weeks. This was in the days before home video players, game consoles, and the Internet. By the ninth day I was bored silly. Then I noticed a Living Bible that *Guideposts* had sent our family. I picked it up and started to read. Wow. In Sunday school they had always used the King James, which I could never understand. But the Living Bible made the text, well, come to life. I remember the stirring I felt in my heart as I finally understood Jesus' amazing teachings. I read all four Gospels and was deep into Paul's letters before I had to go back to school. This was the beginning of my pursuit of God.

One other development on the Scripture front—there are New Testaments that look like magazines. They're called BibleZines. Wisely, the publisher created separate versions for teen girls and teen guys.[6] The girl version looks like a glamour magazine, while the guy version features a skateboarder on front. If this seems like a corruption of God's Holy Word, let me ask you: how many books at your local Barnes and Noble are bound with leather and sprayed with gold leaf? Maybe one of the reasons guys think the Bible is old-fashioned is that it still comes in a package that was designed in the twelfth century.

⟁ THE ROLE OF A MENTOR ⟁

I've shared a forest of ideas in this chapter. But consider this one the giant sequoia: your son would benefit from a godly male mentor.

Christianity has always passed virally from one man to another. Why do you think Jesus personally discipled twelve men? Or consider the example of Paul, who always took a Barnabas, Silas, or Timothy along on his many journeys. It's not that faith *can't* pass from mother to son. But faith that passes from man to man seems to drop deeper roots.

If you are married, your husband is the obvious choice to serve as a spiritual mentor. Show him the studies I cited earlier in this chapter. Help him realize the huge impact he is having on the boy, and encourage him to take a more active role in developing the youngster's faith.

Some husbands feel uncomfortable in this role because they've never been mentored themselves, or they feel they lack Bible knowledge. Your husband needs to realize spiritual mentoring is not necessarily Bible study. It might be as simple as talking openly about his faith in front of the boy. For example, your husband, in the course of conversation, might mention a time he prayed and God answered. Boys who would normally resist a formalized religious lesson are often fascinated when spiritual matters come up naturally (Deut. 6:7).

Ask God how you can encourage your husband to take up this mantle of spiritual leadership. Feel free to nag God about this, but please, don't nag your husband. Mention it once, and then let God convict him of the need.

I realize that in many cases your husband cannot fill this role, either because you are unmarried or because your husband is not a follower of Jesus. In some cases, even Christian husbands are unable or unwilling to serve as a mentor. What do you do then?

Here's my advice: find another male mentor for your son. Pronto.

Ask a godly man in your church to single out your son whenever he sees him. Ask him to do things with your son. This is how I came to Christ: my father was not a disciple of Jesus, but I was won to faith at the age of fifteen by two godly men in my church who got to know me. I know many men who were led to Christ this way.

A good male mentor is hard to find. If you locate one, get out of his way. One time I was asked by a single mother to mentor her thirteen-year-old son. I agreed. The very next day, she and her son were over at our house. The boy challenged me, so I corrected him firmly, just as I would my own son. I didn't yell at him, but I made it clear that such shenanigans were not welcome in the Murrow home. The boy took it in stride, but his mother came unglued. She was very angry that I'd talked to *her son* that way, and she put a quick end to my mentoring of the young man.

Women, you must realize that sweetness and smiles do not a man make. A man matures when he encounters another man who is tougher and more determined than he is. When iron sharpens iron, sparks fly. Consider Jesus, who made it a point to insult not just His enemies but His followers as well. He called His best friend "Satan" and slapped crowds of adoring fans with the tags "perverse" and "wicked"(Matt. 16:23; 17:17; 12:39 NIV). Our discipleship methods often fail with men because they are so nurturing, safe, bookish, and polite.

YOUR TURN

1. When you read that a married woman has a fifty-to-one chance of leading her boys to Christ without the help of her husband, how did you feel?

2. Have you tried to blow a Christian bubble around your family? How is it working?

3. Where do you draw the line between protecting your family from worldly influences and being a scaredy-cat?

4. If you are married, is your husband willing to mentor your boy(s)? If not, whom could you approach about being a godly male mentor for your son(s)?

5. Christianity passes virally from one man to another. In what ways are you regularly exposing your sons to men who have the disease?

TAKE ACTION

Make an appointment for you and your sisters to meet with the Sunday school superintendent and the youth leader. Share some ideas from this book and offer your support.

E I G H T E E N

Reaching All Those Other Guys
(Who Don't Live Under Your Roof)

You want your light to shine before all men—not just the men who share your last name and address. How do you, as a woman, influence all the other men you come into contact with?

Let's begin with some general advice on reaching men. Some of these tips are repeats from earlier chapters. I've gathered them for you in the following list:

- Your goal is to outlive the man you're trying to reach. Your life must look like filet mignon compared to his Kibbles 'n' Bits.
- Beware of the Christian subculture. You don't want to be so heavenly minded you're no earthly good.
- Let your life do the talking. Don't push spiritual conversations unless he brings up the subject.
- A religious life will bore him. If he sees you living an adventurous Christian life that's bearing real fruit, he'll take notice.
- If he asks, have a fresh testimony of how God is working in your life right now—not something that happened to you twenty years ago.

- Stand up for yourself and your faith. When challenged, be respectful but firm.
- Watch for times of crisis. Men change when life forces them to change. Guys are often more open to God when things are going badly (more on this in our next chapter).
- Before ministering to men outside your family, get the advice of your sisters. They can help you avoid the appearance of immorality.

Let's take this one relationship at a time. We'll start with your father.

 **FATHER**

Sharing your faith with Daddy (or step-Daddy) can be awkward. He's always been your teacher, yet now you know something—or should I say Someone—he doesn't. You have so much history together—both bitter and sweet. How do you cut through the thicket of your past and share the truth with him?

Your game plan is the fifth commandment: "Honor your father and your mother." The very best way to draw your father to Christ is to honor him. Show him respect. Ask his advice—and take it. Never make him feel inferior or judged because he does not share your faith.

I don't see a statute of limitations on this command. Even if you're old enough to have grandkids of your own, you're still commanded to honor your parents—even if they don't know Jesus.

What if Dad thinks he's a Christian but doesn't really know the Lord? Same strategy: honor him. Make *him* the religious expert. Ask him to explain spiritual concepts to you. When he says something you find implausible, don't correct him. Keep asking questions. Give him enough rope to hang himself. Don't argue with him—honor him.

As always, prayer is vital. My father was a lapsed Catholic. My mother, sister, and I prayed for his salvation for decades. We honored him as best we could, even when he acted dishonorably. My sister and I had told Dad about Christ several times, but he never responded.

In the months before his death, my father became incapacitated. One day a female caregiver initiated a spiritual conversation. She found my father's heart open, and she led him in a prayer of repentance. I wish I could say he became a model Christian. Still, there was change in his life that we can only attribute to the working of the Spirit. Please, keep praying. God may use you or another woman to lead your father to Christ.

BROTHER

How do you share your faith with the guy who used to put crickets in your lunchbox? The idiot who locked you in the closet under the stairs? The numbskull who snapped your training-bra strap?

The brother-and-sister relationship can be ticklish. You know him so well, yet at times you feel you don't know him at all. How do you share Christ with him?

Let's go to the Scriptures again:

> Therefore, if you are offering your gift at the altar and there remember that your brother has something against you, leave your gift there in front of the altar. First go and be reconciled to your brother; then come and offer your gift. (Matt. 5:23–24 NIV)

You have a gift for your brother. But first you need to be reconciled to him.

Do hard feelings remain? Is there anything you need to get off your chest (that bra-snapping incident, for example)? Whatever your situation, I encourage you to pursue a courageous reconciliation with your brother. Extend him extravagant forgiveness. Deal with the hurts of the past. Humble yourself and see what God does. Your witness will be weakened until things are patched up.

If you enjoy a good relationship with your brother, encourage him as you would any other man. Model a life of joy. Ask great questions. Tell him what God is doing in your life, as the opportunity arises.

Because he's your brother, you have the right to ask him big questions, such as, "Is life turning out the way you planned?" or "You seem so unhappy. What's the matter?" These inquiries not only show concern, but they may open the door to a life-changing conversation.

If your brother comes from out of town for a visit, should you invite him to church? You know your church, and you know your brother. Pray about it. If it seems like a good fit, extend the invitation. Better yet, ask a man to invite him.

⚓ OTHER MALE FAMILY MEMBERS ⚓

How about those other men you're related to—cousins, uncles, stepbrothers, and the like? You are in a unique position to share your faith with these men because there is no suspicion of your motives. Allow me to explain. If a woman builds a relationship with a man outside her family, he may think she has romantic intent. But if you are reaching out to a male relative, there's little likelihood of a misunderstanding.

Again, as you speak with these men, try to get past the pleasantries and ask great questions. Get them talking. Find out how they're *really* doing. You may not be able to get as personal as you would with your brother, but you can go deeper than you would with a stranger. Ask God for a discerning heart and an opportunity to tell your story.

 ## Male Friends

How about outreach to male friends, neighbors, and acquaintances? Now it gets quite tricky.

If you are married, it is not appropriate for you to pray or read the Bible alone with a man who is not your husband. If you are single, it is inappropriate for you to pray or read the Bible alone with a married man. As a Christian woman, you need to avoid even the appearance of impropriety.

The danger lies far beyond mere appearances. When the Holy Spirit quickens our human spirits, it's easy for us to become excited. Two people who share intimacy with their Creator can sometimes misdirect that intimacy into a human relationship. This almost happened to me some years ago.

I was a married man, serving on a foreign missions team with a hurting single woman. (Let's call her Simone.) Simone was contemplating marriage. But as she told me about her boyfriend Bart, it was obvious he was faking his faith in order to win her. We had a couple of talks in which I counseled her strongly against marrying this fellow. We prayed together after chapel one morning. As we prayed, Simone felt the Lord telling her not to marry Bart.

After we got back to the States, Simone contacted me, saying her resolve was slipping. We arranged to meet for lunch. The moment we sat down in the restaurant, I could tell that our closeness was growing too close. God showed me that as a married man, I was about to jump the guardrail, so I backed off.

Avoid these entanglements. If you are married and want to minister to a single man, try to get him a Christian friend. If you want to reach out to a married man, minister to his wife. Build her faith in Christ, and let God work through her. Do we have an understanding?

MALE COWORKERS

Workplace witnessing can be messy. Here your actions are not only governed by God, but they also come under the authority of the employer, your employee code of conduct, the employment laws of your state, and constitutional guarantees of freedom of speech and religion.

I hope I've made it crystal clear that you should only share a verbal witness when men ask for it. This is doubly important on the job. The best workplace testimony is a 1 Peter 3 life: be respectful to the boss, be honest in all your dealings, be loyal to the team, and have a good attitude.

Don't be a manipulator. Don't secretly tune your coworker's radio to the Christian station. Be judicious about adding "hallelujahs" and "praise the Lords" to your conversation. Don't stuff your cubicle with religious kitsch. A single scripture magnet or verse-of-the-day calendar will suffice. Let your coworkers know you have a life beyond church.

Let me reiterate my warning against married-single or married-married entanglements, especially on the job. Not only do they have the potential to hurt you and your loved ones, but you may dishonor the name of Jesus without intending to.

I know of a married male schoolteacher who lived a dynamic life of faith. One day a married female colleague began asking him questions about God. He eventually led the woman to Christ. So far, so good. Then she asked him to teach her the Bible. He jumped at the chance (after all, they were both teachers). The two began meeting an hour before school to study the Scriptures. They kept the classroom door open for all to see. They informed their spouses of the arrangement. Despite their pure motives and extra precautions, it wasn't long before tongues began wagging at school. A weed of suspicion sprouted in both their marriages. The man eventually realized he was on dangerous ground. He stepped aside and arranged for a woman to continue the mentoring process.

Now what about witnessing to your male boss? This is just about the most complicated scenario imaginable. Not only do you have employment laws and lines of authority to deal with, but there is a long history of supervisors having affairs with subordinates. Jealous coworkers may see you as a sycophant.

If a superior initiates a spiritual conversation, be careful. He may be seeking intimacy with you instead of God. The best thing to do is invite him and his wife to church or a couples' Bible study. If he is single, get him connected to a Christian man as soon as possible. Your male boss needs to be discipled by a guy, not by you.

 ## EX-HUSBAND

Okay, how about the ex? Hoo boy. Talk about a tangled vine. I'll offer this simple advice: don't do it alone. You will need the counsel of godly women every step of the way. God bless you.

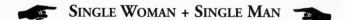 ## SINGLE WOMAN + SINGLE MAN

I think I've covered all the bases, except one. What if you're single and the man you want to reach is single as well? He's not a coworker or a relative. What's next?

You need to realize how sticky this situation can become. You may have zero romantic interest in this guy, but as you share the things of God, he could get the wrong idea. So have an exit plan. Make it clear from the starting gate that this is about Christ, not kissy-face. If the relationship heads that direction, cut it off—even if he is on the cusp of a religious awakening.

If you harbor any romantic feelings for the man you're witnessing to, proceed with extreme caution. You are walking down a well-worn trail of tears. It's called *missionary dating*. Definition: a woman meets an attractive guy who's not a Christian, and the woman decides to win him to Christ so she can have a believer for a boyfriend—or a husband. This strategy seems to make sense. There is such a shortage of single Christian men; why not manufacture one of your own?

Coast Guard rescue swimmers plunge into angry seas to save the lives of people lost in the waves. One of the greatest hazards they face is not the pounding surf or jagged rocks—it's the threat of being pulled underwater by the person they're trying to save.

If you date or marry a man with hopes of saving him later, you will be pulled under. In 2 Corinthians 6:14, Paul commands us to not become yoked to unbelievers. A romantic relationship is a yoke. Marriage is a yoke you can't remove.

You say, "But David, I haven't had a date in eons. I'm so lonely. My church has no single men my age." Friend, that pang of loneliness is a pinprick in your heart compared to the dagger of being permanently yoked to a man who does not know the love of God. If your boyfriend is not walking with Christ, there is only one prudent course of action to take: break up with him.

I want to warn you about a couple of guys. One is named *Pete the predator*. He looks like a Christian. He talks like a Christian. But he is in church for one reason: to stalk women. He knows there's an unlimited supply of lonely single gals under those steeples. Pete likes wholesome girls, and church is the place to find them. Pete is often found in Pentecostal circles. He looks for the ladies who become the most emotional during the worship service, because he has learned they are the most passionate in bed.

Then there's *Fred the fake*. Fred is not as devious as Pete; he simply falls for a Christian woman and pretends to embrace the faith until the rings are on and the rice has been tossed. After a few Sundays, Fred quits going to church and reverts to his true form. Remember Simone, the single woman I was advising to not marry her boyfriend? Poor Simone. She ended up marrying Fred the fake. Last I heard she was quite unhappy.

So how do you identify Pete and Fred? Here are a few tips:

- Remember, love is blind. Once you've fallen for one of these guys, it's very hard to discern his true nature.
- You can't tell from externals. Lee Strobel wrote, "Just because a person may claim to be a Christian, regularly attend church, speak fluent Christianese, and perform good deeds doesn't guarantee that he has truly received Christ and that the Holy Spirit therefore dwells in him."[1]
- Strobel has written a list of fifteen questions you should ask yourself before you date. Here are five of them: Who does he spend his time with? What does he choose to feed his mind? When he talks about the future, is there room for God? Can he describe a specific time or era during which he received Christ's gift of eternal life? If he were put on trial for being a Christian, would there be enough evidence to convict him?[2]
- Ask a godly friend to examine the situation and give an honest opinion. Don't get mad if your friend points out your blind spots.
- If the signs indicate you're dating Fred or Pete, cut it off—before you get hurt.

PROVERBS 22:1 SAYS, "A good name is to be chosen rather than great riches, loving favor rather than silver and gold." I know you desire to see men walking with the Savior. But you must also be wise. There is no instance in the Bible of a woman leading a man outside her family to faith. Use extreme caution in these situations. Your reputation and Christ's are at stake.

YOUR TURN

1. How is your relationship with your dad? Is he walking with Jesus?

2. How about your brothers? Do they know the Lord? Have you ever tried to share your faith with them?

3. How is your witness at work?

4. Do you know a woman who married Pete the predator or Fred the fake? What is her life like?

5. Have you ever gotten close to an inappropriate relationship with a man to whom you were ministering? What happened?

TAKE ACTION

Are you at odds with a man? If so, what step can you take today toward reconciliation?

How to Support a Man
in His Walk with God

You're probably familiar with the sports term *home-field advantage*. Athletes perform better when they're cheered on from the stands. In 2007, every Major League Baseball team (except the Mets) earned more victories at home than they did on the road.

Men gravitate toward whatever is cheering them on. A fellow becomes a workaholic when his boss cheers him on. He performs stupid macho stunts when his buddies cheer him on. He commits adultery when a woman cheers him on.

If you want to see a man growing in faith, you need to cheer louder than worldly tempters do. This chapter will teach you how to pick up your megaphone and drown out the cheers that lead to destruction.

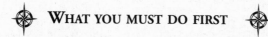

WHAT YOU MUST DO FIRST

Let's say an athlete gets hurt during a game. He's bleeding profusely. What's the first thing his trainer must do? Stop the bleeding. Once the cut is stitched up, he can help the man recover from his injuries and eventually get him back into the game.

The men of our churches are bleeding to death spiritually. In many cases, the women they love have inflicted the wounds.

If you truly want to encourage your man, step one is to stop the bleeding. Put a tourniquet on discouragement, backbiting, and belittling. Squeeze a clamp on your critical tongue. Take a scalpel to your attitude of spiritual superiority. A man cannot come to health in Christ with the woman he loves slashing away at his heart.

Sometimes Christian women, in a well-meaning effort to push their men toward God, end up poisoning the relationship. In her book *Spiritually Single*, Jerri Odell tells the story of a couple named Dan and Jorie.[1] She was a new Christian. He was not yet a believer. Jorie prayed for Dan's salvation every day for two years. One day her prayers were answered: Dan decided to follow Jesus. Tears of joy rolled down Jorie's face. She was so happy—for a little while. But Dan did not live up to her idea of a Christian, and she was quick to express her disappointment.

Jorie said, "If Dan was working on his computer, I would make a snide remark about not having time for God but always having time for work. If he decided to skip church for a football game, I would be furious and not speak to him for days. I made so many demands he finally told me he was giving up on this Christian thing. There was no way he could live up to all my expectations."

Dan never returned to church. The marriage almost ended in divorce. In fact, Dan found acceptance in the arms of another woman because he could not endure Jorie's constant criticism of his spiritual inadequacies.

Jorie is not the only woman who unloads on her spiritually lagging husband. I've heard of women carving up their men with words like these: "Why can't you pray like the preacher can?" Others say, "How come you read so slow in Sunday school?" *Cut. Slash. Stab.* If you want to send your man running from a life of faith, point out his spiritual inadequacies.

Sometimes Christian women get together to rag on their men. They swap *my-husband-is-worse-than-your-husband* stories. So what's the harm in this? What men don't know can't hurt them, right?

When I was learning to downhill ski, my instructor said, "Turn your head and your skis will follow." Be careful: if you're tearing down your man behind his back, your relationship will follow your caustic words—straight downhill. If you've been dissing your men, I encourage you to ask God's forgiveness this very moment. Choose to speak only words that build up your men—even when they're not around.

One time Gina and I led a couples' Bible study in our home. Eduardo and Rita (names changed) were regulars. One time I asked Eduardo to look up a scripture. When he couldn't find it fast enough, Rita took the Bible from him and—with a dramatic sigh— had the passage lassoed in 8.3 seconds. She handed the Bible back to her embarrassed husband with a look of triumph. Rita had used God's two-edged sword to publicly emasculate her man.

Then I learned the rest of the story. Eduardo was a very critical husband. Though he was quite charming in public, he constantly belittled his wife at home. Rita saw this as her chance to get the better of Eduardo—and to make *him* feel like the dummy.

Rita won the battle, but she lost the war. Eduardo never returned to our group. Eventually he left the church. The marriage was destroyed. I'm not saying this single incident was the cause, but the enemy used it to cut off Eduardo from his source of Christian fellowship and support.

Women, you must never use your spiritual superiority to get even with your husband. Instead, follow the command of Paul: "Do nothing out of selfish ambition or vain conceit, but in humility consider others better than yourselves" (Phil. 2:3 NIV). This is the heart of submission—treat your husband as better than yourself, even if you are more skilled in faith practices.

BUSTED!

Your man will not grow in faith until he conquers the sins that bind him. You can help—by making sure he gets busted.

Men who harbor hidden sins usually want to be caught. They're often careless about leaving clues because deep down they're hoping someone will arrest their fall.

When you discover evidence that a man is sinning, choose your next move carefully. Read Matthew 18:15–17. If the sin is directed against you, do as the scripture says and confront the man privately. Let him know you love him and you want him to live a victorious life. David Augsburger calls this *carefronting.*[2]

The one you *carefront* may initially recoil from the rebuke, but many men eventually come to appreciate it. Deep down every man wants to grow up, and a woman who lovingly opposes his immaturity does him a service.

If a man is still unrepentant, let him hit bottom. Don't cushion his fall. Stop giving him money. Don't bail him out of jail. Let the prodigal find his way to the pigsty. Like Jonah, men often find God in the darkest depths.

Funny thing about men: they often begin their spiritual pilgrimage in response to a crisis. A disease, a business failure, or the loss of a loved one can focus a man on eternity. The Lord does not send these afflictions, but He uses them to draw men to Himself. As a woman, your tendency is to comfort the afflicted. But if your man is in a crisis, too much comfort may work against the purposes of God. Let your man stew in his own juices unless he asks for help.

Now, what if a man is sinning, but that sin is not directed against you? Let's say you have a male coworker who regales you every Monday morning with tales about the wild parties he attended over the weekend. Since he is not sinning against you personally, you have no standing to confront him. Your best bet is not to preach or push but pray. Ask God to change his heart. If his obscenity-laced descriptions become overwhelming, just tell him in great detail what you did over the weekend. Start with your women's Sunday school class. That should shut him up.

𝄃 FAN THE FLAME 𝄃

Moving on to happier thoughts . . . let's say your man is showing interest in the things of God. How can you fan the flame?

Of course there are the usual responses: pray with him, read the Bible, share devotions. Sometimes these work; sometimes they don't. (We'll see why later in this chapter.)

The absolute best thing you can do is get your man into the presence of other godly men. Proverbs 27:17 says, "As iron sharpens iron, so one man sharpens another" (NIV). I can't overstate how important it is to help him find a spiritual father and a band of brothers to encourage him in his walk. Remind him that the Christian life is more like football than golf. To really enjoy it, he needs a team around him.

HE NEEDS TO BE NEEDED

Here's one thing to keep in mind: men need to be needed. I mentioned this way back in chapter 4, but it bears repeating in the context of encouragement. Guys are happiest in church when they have a unique skill to offer to God. I speak from personal experience.

Since 1983, I've worked in the television industry. Through most of the 1980s and '90s, my video know-how was virtually useless in church. Not anymore. With the installation of big screens in sanctuaries, video skills are now in demand. It gives me great satisfaction to use my talents for the cause of Christ.

So what is your man good at? Where do his passions lie? Is there a way he can deploy his skills toward kingdom work? Help him find a way to contribute to the body of Christ—even if he is not yet *in Christ*.

ENCOURAGE HIS INTEREST IN THE BIBLE

Getting a man to read the Bible with you can be tricky. Here's an approach that probably won't work: "Hey Jim, let's start reading the Bible together every morning." This sounds to Jim like he's enrolling for a 6:30 a.m. class.

Instead, appeal to his curiosity. "Hey Jim, I was reading something unusual in the Gospels the other day. People always think of Jesus as the Prince of Peace. But I found a passage that says the disciples carried weapons—and Jesus approved of it. Would you like to hear it?" (FYI, it's in Luke 22.)

If Jim says yes, grab your Bible and read it to him. Who knows, it might prompt a discussion and further reading later on.

If your guy is agreeable, pick up one of those devotional booklets you find in the church lobby. My wife and I read these for years, and eventually we expanded to reading the suggested Bible passage included with the devotion.

Your guy may not be the most studious type, so he may never graduate to full-on Bible study. That's okay. Jesus told us to make disciples, not seminarians. Pastor Dan Jarrell said, "As long as you're flying, your altitude doesn't usually matter. It's your trajectory that really counts."[3]

HELP HIM PRAY

How can you help a man pray? Here is Jesus' advice:

> When you pray, say: Our Father in heaven, hallowed be Your name.
> Your kingdom come. Your will be done on earth as it is in heaven.
> Give us day by day our daily bread. And forgive us our sins, for we
> also forgive everyone who is indebted to us. And do not lead us into
> temptation, but deliver us from the evil one. (Luke 11:2–4)

That's our model. Simple and straightforward. Fifty-nine words. Can be prayed in less than thirty seconds. Unfortunately, we've taken this economical model of prayer and morphed it into something God may have never intended.

I think a lot of guys are discouraged from praying because they feel their orations aren't long or fancy enough. As a young man, I can remember sitting in church, hearing tales of some great man of prayer who spent four to six hours on his knees every day—before sunrise! Such accounts were meant to encourage more prayer, but they always left me feeling inadequate, like I was a disappointment to God if I wasn't wearing out a pair of Levi's every month.

Whenever groups of men and women pray aloud together, the women almost always pray more. They pray longer. Their prayers are more eloquent and well formed. Why is this?

By now you understand the verbal agility of the female brain. But it's not just raw fluency that gives women a leg up. You may have never noticed this, but evangelicals use a strange language when they talk to God. I call it *prayer-speak*. It's an insider's code. Women and pastors are eloquent in this language. Some laymen eventually master it after many years in church. But to your average guy, it's as foreign as ancient Greek.

Prayer-speak is a nonstop speech to God, with frequent repetitions of His blessed, holy name, punctuated by the word *just*. I recently prayed with a woman who was fluent in prayer-speak. Read her opening statement aloud, quickly as you can, and see if it doesn't sound familiar to your ears:

> Father God, we just thank You for this day, blessed Father, and we just ask You to be with us, Father, and we just want to praise Your holy name for the many blessings You bestow upon us, Lord, and Father, we just ask You to touch us, Father, touch us deeply, and Father, we just come to You now, bringing our petitions before the throne of grace, dear God, and Father . . .

There are several versions of prayer-speak, including King James prayer-speak ("We thank Thee, O Lord"), Pentecostal prayer-speak ("Hallelujah Jeeee-zus"), and mainline prayer-speak (sloooow and sleeeepy).

Now, I realize that most prayer-speakers are sincere Christians who want to communicate with God. I'm not accusing anyone of hypocrisy or deception. But prayer-speak is having an unintended side effect: it's intimidating men into silence.

Sam sits in church listening to longtime Christians communicating with God in prayer-speak. He thinks, *I'd like to pray, but I can't pray like that.* It's hard enough for Sam to have a conversation with someone who doesn't talk back (audibly). Requiring him to do so in a foreign dialect raises the bar too high.

You may be thinking, *Sam doesn't have to use prayer-speak. He can talk to God however he wants.* You know this. I know this. But Sam doesn't know this. He wants to fit in, and if the rest of the group uses a prayer code, he feels like a dork when he can't match it. Rather than be embarrassed, he keeps his trap shut.

Are you familiar with prayer-speak? Perhaps you are a native speaker. If so, I encourage you to do the following:

- Think before you pray. Much of the excess verbiage in our prayers are snippets of Christianese we've learned in church. Look at the woman's prayer I quoted above. Did she really say anything to God, or was she simply parroting familiar churchy phrases?
- Shorten your prayers. As God leads you to say something, say it. Then yield the floor to someone else. A heartfelt, ten-second prayer is more powerful than ten minutes of "vain repetitions" (Matt. 6:7).
- When you pray aloud, talk like a normal person: "God, this makes me so mad!" or "Father, I love my new job. Thanks." Or "Jesus, there's this woman at work who's driving me nuts."
- Remember, Christ isn't looking for elegant prayers; He wants relevant prayers (Luke 18:9–14).

When a man hears prayers that sound like real conversation, he'll be encouraged to pray himself.

⚓ HUBBY, WILL YOU PRAY WITH ME? ⚓

Would you like your husband to pray with you? Most women would. Yet few couples consistently pray together—even those who attend church regularly. Pastor Larry Keefauver wrote, "For the hundreds of times I heard wives sigh, 'I wish my husband would pray with me,' I rarely hear any husband express that desire."[4]

After reading this quote, I asked an audience of about one hundred Christian guys, "Have you prayed with your wife this week?"

About a dozen men raised their hands. Then I asked, "Would you like to?" Nearly every hand in the room shot up.

Why the disconnect between men's actions and desires? Let me explain it this way: I know a lot of men who love to play basketball. But these guys would shake in their Reeboks if given the chance to go one-on-one against an NBA superstar like Carmelo Anthony or LeBron James. It would be way too intimidating.

Ladies, when it comes to praying aloud, women are the superstars, flying to the hoop of grace and slam-dunking their requests before God. Thanks to their highly verbal brains and prayer-speak fluency, women literally intimidate their men into silence.

For years, this insecurity kept me from praying with my wife. Oh, we tried. We would kneel by the bedside. There would be a brief period of silence, and then it began. My highly verbal wife would open the floodgates of her heart, gushing a torrent of words toward the heavenly throne. Five or ten minutes would elapse with hardly a breath, comma, or period.

Then, silence. It was my turn. As a man, I felt I had to match her length and intensity. I could never do it. My prayers felt short and stubby after my wife's lengthy epistle. Deep in my heart I felt outclassed. So I gave up.

If you are praying with a man, please start in silence. Give him the first word. Then as you take your turn, match his length and cadence. I know you just want to rush into God's presence and tell Him everything. But you will make your man feel inadequate if your prayers sound better than his. Instead of lifting a speech to God, just offer a brief sentence or two, and then wait for the Spirit's prompting before speaking again.

One more thing: my wife and I have begun salting our daily conversation with spontaneous prayer. We talk to God as a third person as we're walking or driving or shopping. No eyes closed or head bowed. Your man may be more willing to pray if he can do it on the spur of the moment, as the Spirit leads. It feels less religious and more real to me.

If the man you're married to still won't pray with you, there's one more thing you can try. According to one study, married couples who pray together are 90 percent more likely to report higher satisfaction with their sex life than couples who do not pray together. Also, women who pray with their partner tend to be more orgasmic.[5] If the promise of better sex doesn't drive your husband to his knees, nothing will.

 ## BEWARE THE PRAYER MUSHROOM

It's not just what we say but what we do with our bodies during prayer that can send men over the edge. Have you heard of a *prayer mushroom*? You know what I'm talking about: Brother Alex asks for prayer and soon a crowd has gathered around him, placing their hands all over his body. With every head bowed and every eye closed, Alex must sit stock still while prayers go on for five, ten, fifteen minutes or longer. There are long silences, and suddenly—a prayer wreck—two people begin speaking at once. Someone finally has the courage to utter a forceful *amen*, but then Brother Alex may have to stand up and hug a bunch of strangers.

Why do guys fear the mushroom? Men's ministry expert Dan Schaeffer reminds us, "Women equate closeness with safety. Men equate personal space with safety."[6] You see this whenever men gather in an auditorium. They spread out like marbles dropped on a kitchen floor. But women sit in tight little knots, with hardly an open seat between them.

A prayer mushroom is an unnatural experience for a man. His instinct is to flee. His testosterone makes it hard to sit still. And having strange hands all over his body is worse than having a squirrel loose in his jockeys.

Plus, prayer mushrooms freak out the other guys. When we call Brother Alex forward to lay hands on him, the rest of the men in the congregation are watching. They keep their prayer requests to themselves, because they don't want to end up *under the mushroom*. Pretty soon you have got twelve women and one old man coming forward for prayer.

Some men's groups are experimenting with an alternative to the prayer mushroom. It's called a *prayer force*. Brother Alex sits or stands in the middle of a semicircle. The men step forward and pray for him one at a time. Some may lay hands on Alex. Others may just pray from where they stand. This format is less intimidating to guys and can be tremendously powerful in men's lives. (For a demonstration of a prayer force at work, visit my Web site, www.churchformen.com.)

 ## Speak his love language

If you want to encourage your man, do it according to his love language. Every person has one, according to Dr. Gary Chapman. He has identified five of them: *words of affirmation, quality time, receiving gifts, acts of service,* and *physical touch.*[7]

My love language is that last one, so my wife makes sure to give me a hug whenever she sees me. If I'm discouraged, she comes alongside me or takes my hand. If I'm stressed out, she gives me a neck rub. For me, touch is more encouraging than any pep talk.

 ## Let him lead

If you step back and allow your husband to be the spiritual leader in your home, I can guarantee you this: he will not lead the way you think it should be done. He may not join a Bible study, lead family devotions, or listen to Christian radio in the car. At some point you will think, *I could do things better.* Your husband knows this as well. This is why most guys are more than happy to let their wives manage the family's religious portfolio. It is only as women voluntarily step back, grit their teeth, and allow their spiritually inept husbands to lead that men will take on this role.

What if you step back and your husband still won't lead? Step back anyway. If you grow impatient and take the reins, your man will never rise to the challenge. And your son(s) will see the gospel as a woman's thing.

⊤ A WORD OF CAUTION ⊤

As I wrap up, here's a suggestion that's going to drive you crazy. I started this chapter by challenging you to cheer for your men. Now, I have a warning: don't overdo it. If a woman cheers too enthusiastically, a man may feel as though he's her project. A woman who gushes over her man's spiritual progress can sometimes spook him.

Once again, Christ shows us the way. One day a fellow approached Jesus, promising to follow Him anywhere. Christ could have said, "Wow, that's great. We're glad you're here. Bartholomew has a new disciple packet and coffee mug for you." But look how Jesus addressed the potential recruit: "Foxes have dens, and birds have nests. But the Son of Man doesn't have a place to call His own" (Matt. 8:20 CEV). Modern translation: *Follow Me, and you'll be homeless the rest of your life.* He then wheeled around and rebuked another would-be disciple for wanting to bury his father.

It's an honor to serve the King of kings. It's good for us to rejoice when a lost sheep is found, but sometimes we overdo it with men. We give a man the impression that the gospel revolves around him and his personal salvation. But every man truly longs to be part of a great movement that's focused on God—not on him.

Y O U R   T U R N

1. Have you ever cheered too enthusiastically (or pushed too hard) for a man's spiritual growth? What happened?

2. Have you ever confronted a man about his sin? What happened?

3. Do you like prayer mushrooms?

4. Have you ever emasculated a man spiritually? Share the story with your sisters.

5. Have you ever tried praying or reading the Bible with a man? How did it go?

T A K E   A C T I O N

Get together with your sisters and practice praying without prayer-speak. See if you can pray without repeating God's name or using the word *just*.

T W E N T Y

Your Mission . . .
Should You Decide to Accept It

Our journey has reached its end. This is summit day, when we stand atop the mountain and enjoy a bird's-eye view of the terrain we've covered in our previous nineteen chapters. Details fade; only broad outlines remain. Here's a twenty-thousand-foot overview of *How Women Help Men Find God*:

- Jesus was an expert at reaching men, but today's church culture unwittingly alienates many guys.
- Once a woman understands the chasm that has developed between men and church, she can bridge the gap in two ways:

  1. She can help her congregation become more welcoming to guys.
  2. She can sharpen her personal witness to men and boys.

Did you enjoy your mountaintop moment? Good. So did Moses. But eventually he had to leave Sinai, carrying a fresh revelation of God down to the people. And so must you. Here are five ways you can make me proud:

- Talk about the gender gap to your Christian friends. Most churchgoing people have never realized we're short of men and boys.
- Stand up for guy stuff. Be a vocal supporter of any effort to make the church more welcoming to men.
- Support men's ministry, men's activities, male-only events, and bands of brothers. Resist the urge to feel left out when men-only opportunities are announced.
- Gather a circle of sisters to work on this issue in your church.
- Most importantly: search your heart. Make sure your motives are pure.

What did I mean by that last one? Sometimes Christians want the right thing—but for the wrong reason.

 ### SEVEN QUESTIONS FOR YOU

As a final challenge, I'm going to ask seven tough, personal questions. These are not designed to embarrass you but to help you align your heart with God's agenda, rather than your own.

1. Why Do You Go to Church?

I once heard a shockingly frank radio interview with the pastor of a large mainline congregation. Although I don't have his exact quote, it went something like this:

> Hundreds of our members come to church not because they want to meet with God, but because it's the one constant in their life.

Society is changing, morals are changing, and technology is changing. Their job is changing, their bodies are changing, and their relationships are changing.

But church is the one thing that's never supposed to change. These folks come to church in order to participate in a comforting ritual that has changed little since childhood. This is why people go ballistic over small changes in the order of worship. When I announce a new initiative, I see pained expressions all over the sanctuary. Their eyes plead with me: church is my root system; don't uproot me.

A lot of nice people go to church for the wrong reasons. It's an anchor. A link to the past. A family time. They love the ritual. It's where their friends go. They enjoy a feeling of warmth and connectedness to God and His people.

If this describes you, then you are using the church instead of allowing God to use you. If you really want to see the men you love transformed, you must be transformed. That leads us to our next question.

2. Are You a Transformed Follower of Jesus?

Is there a moment in time when you died and Christ began living through you? When you were truly changed? If the answer is no (or I don't know), we may have found the heart of the matter.

One time I bought a computer system. I spent almost an hour setting up the tower, monitor, keyboard, mouse, printer, USB hub, and scanner. Everything worked—but I could not get the main computer to fire up. I spent another hour on the phone waiting for tech support. I was nearing the point of on-hold-music insanity when my wife walked into the room. She knelt behind the computer and gave the power cord a firm push into its socket. The system roared to life.

Ladies, your witness to men may lack power because you're not truly plugged into the source of all spiritual power—Jesus Himself. You may think you are. There might have been a time as a girl you prayed to receive Jesus into your heart. Or you may have a religious pedigree that traces back to St. Augustine. But you're not completely sure Christ's power is flowing through you today. How can you be certain?

If you have even the slightest doubt about your status before God, please read this word from Christ very carefully: "I am the vine, and you are the branches. If you stay joined to me, and I stay joined to you, then you will produce lots of fruit. But you cannot do anything without me" (John 15:5 CEV).

That's the test. If you are joined to Him, your life *will* be producing much fruit. But if you are not joined to Him, you will accomplish nothing.

Take an honest look at your Christian life. Are you producing real, lasting fruit? Or are you accomplishing very little? Are lives changing as a result of your ministry, or are you a whirlwind of religious activity? Based on the standard of Jesus, can you confidently say you are joined to the Vine? Are you plugged into the Source of all power?

If you cannot answer these questions with an unequivocal *yes*, then your next step is critical. Put this book down and call a friend who is definitely joined to the Vine. Her face probably just popped into your mind. Do it now. Admit your doubt and ask her to explain what it means to be connected to Christ. Humble yourself, and God will lift you up.

Don't read another sentence until you are certain you are joined to the Vine. God may need to change you before He can change the men you care about.

3. Why Do You Want Your Man in Church?

You thought the last question was hard. I double-dog dare you to search your heart and tell me the *real* reason you want that man in the pew.

Women constantly try to perfect their lives. (That's why gals buy most of the self-help books and magazines.) So it follows that some women would treat the Holy Spirit like another therapy that promises to beautify, simplify, or edify their own lives.

Donna's true motive for wanting her husband in church is to relieve her embarrassment. She's tired of sitting alone, feeling inferior to her friends whose husbands go to church. Donna feels like a misfit—she can't socialize with the singles' group, but she feels out of place at couples' events. If only her husband would start coming to church, her stock would rise in the eyes of her friends.

Alena wants her son in church because he's always doing risky things. He parties all night. He rides motorcycles without a helmet. He may be smoking pot. But she believes if her son knew Jesus, all these risky behaviors would melt away. Christ would put him on the straight and narrow.

Rhonda is praying that her boss becomes a Christian because she thinks he would be nicer to her. He'd stop being so critical of her work. He'd give her Sundays off.

Ladies, if you see the church as a spiritual gym that shapes men up: *repent*. Christ did not die a horrible death on the cross so you could have the perfect husband, son, or boss. Christianity is not a rock tumbler that knocks off a man's rough edges, polishes him up, and delivers him to you soft and pretty. If this is your expectation, you are guilty of self-worship.

Paul Coughlin speaks in churches around the country and has met many Christian women who see the church as a domesticating force. "I'm left with the sinking feeling that [women's] real motive for going to church is so that man of theirs will 'get his act together.' If this is true, church isn't about an intimate relationship with God, but about keeping Christian men in line, which is to say, domesticated, by female standards. Men will go back to church when this mind-set is called what it is: manipulation."[1]

John Eldredge asks women, "What's the pure motive for wanting a man to go to church? Because God has a great battle for him to fight and an adventure for him to live, and you are willing and ready for him to find it. No matter what the cost may be to you. That is Eve repenting at the deepest level."[2]

Be careful what you pray for. If your man truly comes to know Jesus, what's to keep him from becoming *harder* to live with? As a Christian, your boss might make you work every Sunday so he can worship. Your husband might become a churchaholic and be gone four nights a week. Your risk-taking son might move to a persecuted country to support an underground church.

I ask you again: Why do you want your man in church? For his benefit, or for yours?

4. Have You Ever Told God Exactly What You Want?

Before Jesus helped a needy person, He would often ask a question when the answer was blindingly obvious. Speaking of blind, one time a pair of sightless men accosted Him, shouting for mercy. Jesus stopped and called them over. Then He asked, "What do you want Me to do for you?"

Duh! They were blind. Why didn't Jesus skip the interview and get down to business?

There's something about *asking* that moves God to action. The Father already knows your every need (Matt. 6:32), yet the Bible tells us, "You do not have because you do not ask" (James 4:2).

So tell me: have you ever asked God specifically for your men's hearts? Have you ever sat down and told Jesus *exactly* what you want? The need may seem obvious to you, but the Lord wants to hear it from your lips.

If you've never done this, take a moment right now. Tell the Lord exactly what you want, clearly, and in faith believe He will answer.

5. Is Your Congregation Man-Friendly?

Now that you know what resonates with men, how does your church measure up? Is there a healthy masculine spirit in your congregation? The sense that God is at work? A risk-taking culture where anything is possible? Are there plenty of enthusiastic, active laymen? Is your pastor the kind of person men follow?

What about opportunities for men? Are there ministries that take advantage of guy skills? Are there spiritual fathers leading bands of brothers?

If you can answer yes to most of these questions, congratulations. Your church gets it. You have found that rare congregation that truly cares about men.

6. If Your Church Is Not Man-Friendly, Is There Any Realistic Hope of Change?

Let's say you gathered a band of like-minded sisters and tried to influence your church culture. Do you honestly think it would do any good? Can you see your church becoming the kind of fellowship where men and boys thrive?

I would encourage you to try. Remember, small changes can produce big results.

7. If There Is Little Hope of Change, What Do You Think God Would Have You Do?

You can stick with your church. You're comfortable there. I usually advise Christians to bloom where they are planted.

But if you're planted in a church with no vision to reach men, and you think change is unlikely, then consider your next step very carefully.

Way back in chapter 1, I told you about my crisis of faith. Well, here's the rest of the story. My simple boredom with church services had metastasized into a cancer that was devouring my soul. My devotional life was dry as a stone in the desert. Temptations raged. I sat through worship like a zombie, unable to pray or even sing.

Desperate for answers, my wife and I started visiting other churches, hoping to discover some new ideas to bring home to our congregation. We were not *church hopping*. But one Sunday we visited a fast-growing church that met in a gym. Ten minutes into the service, I was completely undone by the presence of God. For the first time since Promise Keepers, I felt the pleasure of worshiping Christ in the presence of enthusiastic men. The energy in the room could have powered a small city. The pastor's straightforward message pierced my heart like an arrow. I had walked into that gym questioning my faith; I walked out ready to take on the world.

Minutes after the service was over, Gina and I had the big conversation:

DAVID: Well, what did you think?
GINA: I really liked it. How about you?
DAVID: Oh man, I loved it. I'm ready to join. Are you?
GINA: (surprised) Well . . . I'm reluctant to leave our friends behind.
DAVID: Pray about it. We won't go without your blessing.

So Gina cried a little and prayed a lot. After the second visit, it was apparent that God was calling us to pick up our mats and walk. We joined three weeks later.

And the Murrows lived happily ever after—*not*. Leaving our old church was like a death in the family. Gina's social network disintegrated. She had trouble making friends in our new congregation. So did our kids. They bounced in and out of youth group. The evil one stepped up his attacks on our family.

But that pain has produced lasting gain. There's much laughter and joy these days in the Murrow house. My faith and that of my children has never been stronger. To my surprise, God has given me a ministry with international reach. And you hold in your hands a book that would have never been written if we hadn't made that move.

In twenty-four years of marriage, Gina has given me many gifts. But none was sweeter than her willingness to put her husband's spiritual needs first. She turned her back on relationships and comfort for my sake, but now she's reaping bushels of joy. She has a kind, loving husband who smiles a lot. Her marriage has never been stronger. She has found great friends. As a bonus, God gave her an expanding ministry that's changing the lives of dozens of women.

I tell this story with the utmost reluctance. I am no advocate of church hopping. But if your congregation is tranquilizing its men, it may be time for a bold, risky move. Not only for your man's spiritual health but also for your own.

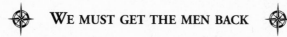

✦ WE MUST GET THE MEN BACK ✦

OK, no more tough questions. You've been challenged enough. Let me wrap up our time together with a pep talk—the kind Jesus gave His disciples in Matthew 10.

If you decide to fight for men and boys, you will face opposition. Much of it will come from your fellow Christians. Crazy, isn't it? Everyone would like to see more guys on Sunday. But the moment a church opens its heart to men, the battle rages. Why is this?

The evil one is frightened of men. He'll fight tooth and nail to keep them on the bench. Any honest reading of church history finds that its most aggressive champions have been courageous men. Women have also played an indispensable role, but as a group they cannot compare to men when it comes to missionary zeal.

History is clear: whenever laymen have returned to church, it has grown in size and influence. Involved laymen are a solid predictor of church health and growth. Simply put, if the men are alive, the church is alive. But if males are passive, demoralized, or bored, you can start planning the congregation's funeral.

Anthropologists note that no religion in history has advanced without the robust participation and leadership of men. When men stop believing, the faith disappears. Why do you think the state churches in Europe are nearing extinction? Why are mainline denominations imploding before our eyes? Their dynamic young men gave up decades ago. Today they're dominated by old women, who provide hospice care for sick and dying institutions.

We must get the men back. You're fighting for so much more than your man's salvation, your personal happiness, or a more peaceful home. Nothing less than the future of the church is at stake.

For years we've called men back to the church. Dear readers, it's time to call our churches back to men.

~

I WANT TO equip you to win this battle. I've established two Web sites and stocked them with the ammunition you need.

My newest site is www.speakingofmen.com. Think of this as a *Dear Abby* for Christian women. You can ask me any question about men, and I'll post the answer for all to see (and yes, I read the questions myself). You'll also find helpful tips, links, and resources that can help you sharpen your outreach. Doesn't it make sense to get guy advice from a guy?

My other site can be found at www.churchformen.com. This site is helpful to church planters and leaders who want to make their congregations more magnetic to men. It's worth a look.

Y O U R   T U R N

If you have the guts, ask each other the seven tough questions in this chapter.

1. Why do you go to church?

2. Are you a transformed follower of Jesus?

3. Why do you want your man in church?

4. Have you ever told God exactly what you want?

5. Is your church man-friendly?

6. If your church isn't man-friendly, is there any realistic hope of change?

7. If there is little hope of change, what do you think God would have you do?

T A K E   A C T I O N

Do you have your circle of sisters yet? I promised to keep bugging you until you do.

NOTES

Introduction

1. The Gallup Poll, May 2–4, 2004, as cited on www.galluppoll.com. Ninety percent of respondents claimed belief in God. Only 4 percent claimed not to. This number has remained virtually unchanged over the past seventy years. Women are slightly more likely to answer in the affirmative than men.

2. Barna Research Online, "Women Are the Backbone of Christian Congregations in America," 6 March 2000, www.barna.org. 83 percent of men polled claimed to be Christians.

3. Thom S. Rainer, *Surprising Insights from the Unchurched and Proven Ways to Reach Them* (Grand Rapids: Zondervan, 2001), 83. Rainer found that "wives were the most influential in reaching the unchurched."

Chapter 1: Where Have All the Good Men Gone?

1. Lyle E. Schaller, *It's a Different World: the Challenge for Today's Pastor* (Nashville: Abingdon Press, 1987), 61–62.

2. Nancy Pearcey, *Total Truth: Liberating Christianity from Its Cultural Captivity* (Wheaton, IL: Crossway, 2004), chapter 12, endnote #4, 441.

3. Barna, "Women Are the Backbone of Christian Congregations in America," 6 March 2000, www.barna.org.

4. I got this figure at a gathering of men's ministry leaders convened by Man in the Mirror in Orlando, Florida, in August 2005. Although I know of no formal study, these experts estimated that only about 10 percent of the congregations in their denominations had any kind of active men's ministry. (Some thought 10 percent was actually a high estimate. No one believed the figure was over 10 percent.)

5. As far as I know, no one has ever researched this number, but as I've spoken around the country, I ask my audiences what percentage of churches they think offer women's and children's ministries. No one guesses below ninety percent. Many people think it's 99 or 100 percent.

6. Barna, "Women Are the Backbone of Christian Congregations in America."

7. Rebecca Barnes and Lindy Lowry: "Special Report: The American Church in Crisis." From *Outreach* magazine, May/June 2006. Posted at: http://www.christianity today.com/outreach/articles/americanchurchcrisis.html.

8. I came up with this figure by taking the U.S. Census 2000 numbers for total married adults and overlaying Barna Research's year 2000 percentages of male-versus-female attendance at weekly worship services. The figures suggest at least 24.5 million married women attend church on a given weekend, but only 19 million married men attend. That's 5.5 million more women, or 22.5 percent. The actual number may be even higher, because married people attend church in much greater numbers than singles.

9. David Murrow, *Why Men Hate Going to Church* (Nashville: Thomas Nelson, 2004).

Chapter 2: Man Laws vs. Church Laws

1. To further shed light on my poll results, note that about a third of men declined to participate. Those who responded were undoubtedly the more relational and outgoing men since they were willing to speak to a polltaker. These are the same men who would probably be more comfortable in a church setting.

2. Barna Research Online, "Women Are the Backbone of Christian Congregations in America," 6 March 2000, www.barna.org.

3. Ibid.

4. Ibid. Also see Albert L. Winseman, "Religion and Gender: A Congregation Divided," 3 December 2002, Gallup Tuesday Briefing, Religion and Values Content Channel, www.gallup.com.

5. Surveys show that in the U.S., atheists, freethinkers (a form of atheism), agnostics, Muslims, Buddhists, Jews, and *no religion* all attract more male adherents, according to The American Religious Identification Survey, Graduate Center, City University of New York, 2001, exhibit 11. Results are a combination of the 1990 and 2001 studies.

6. Nancy Pearcey, *Total Truth: Liberating Christianity from Its Cultural Captivity* (Wheaton, IL: Crossway, 2004), 69.

7. Craig LeMoult, "Why So Few Male Nurses?" Columbia News Service, 18 April 2006, http://jscms.jrn.columbia.edu/cns/2006-04-18/lemoult-malenurses/, accessed 31 August 2007.

Chapter 3: The House of Horrors

1. James Dobson, *Bringing Up Boys* (Wheaton: Tyndale, 2001), 25, 26.

2. Mark I. Pinsky, "Saint Flanders," *Christianity Today*, 5 February 2001.

3. Mark D. Jordan, "What Attracts Gay Men to the Catholic Priesthood?" *Boston Globe*, 3 May 2002, Section A, 23. Richard Sipe, who has studied the sexuality of priests for twenty-five years, also says at least a third of Catholic bishops are gay.

4. J. L. King with Karen Hunter, *On the Down Low: A Journey into the Lives of "Straight" Black Men Who Sleep with Men* (New York: Harlem Moon, 2005), 82–83.

5. Ministry Today Magazine online. Podcast, 5 March 2007. Also see Michael Stevens, *Straight Up: The Church's Official Response to the Epidemic of Downlow Living* (Lake Mary, FL: Creation House, 2007).

6. Jesse Ventura, as quoted at the American Atheists Web site. http://www.atheists.org/flash.line/ventura1.htm. Accessed 20 September 2007.

7. Paul Coughlin, *No More Christian Nice Guy: When Being Nice—Instead of Good—Hurts Men, Women and Children* (Minneapolis: Bethany House, 2005), 18.

8. Personal conversation with Pastor Mark Gungor, Santa Ana, CA, 14 June 2007.

9. Keith Naughton, "Zero Sum Game," *Newsweek*, 26 November 2001, 63.

10. Sabrina D. Black, *Can Two Walk Together? Encouragement for Spiritually Unbalanced Marriages* (Chicago: Moody Publishers, 2002), 194.

11. Dr. Kevin Leman, author of *Sheet Music (Uncovering the Secrets of Sexual Intimacy in Marriage)*. www.lemanbooksandvideos.com. Used by permission.

12. Nancy Wray Gegoire, endorsement of *Why Men Hate Going to Church*, inside cover.

Chapter 4: The Stars vs. the Scrubs

1. Anne and Bill Moir, *Why Men Don't Iron* (New York: Citadel Press, 1999), 116.

2. Ibid., 114–18.

3. Mike Bergman, "Majority of Undergrads and Graduate Students Are Women, Census Bureau Reports." *U.S. Census Bureau News*, 19 December, 2006.

Chapter 5: How We Lose Most of Our Boys

1. "LifeWay Research Uncovers Reasons 18 to 22 Year Olds Drop Out of Church," PowerPoint presentation accompanying study, available at the LifeWay Web site, http://www.lifeway.com/lwc/article_main_page/0,1703, A=165949&M=200906,00.html, accessed 12 September 2007.

2. Peg Tyre, "The Trouble with Boys," *Newsweek*, 30 January 2006, 46.

Chapter 6: How the Grinch Stole Youth Group

1. Beth Redman and Matt Redman, "Let My Words Be Few," Copyright © 2000 Thankyou Music (PRS) (adm. worldwide by EMI CMG Publishing excluding Europe which is adm. by kingswaysongs.com) All rights reserved.

2. Dr. Christian Smith, National Study of Youth and Religion, conducted at the University of North Carolina, Chapel Hill.

3. Paul Hill, David Anderson, and Roland Martinson, *Coming of Age: Exploring the Spirituality and Identity of Younger Men* (Minneapolis: Augsburg, 2006), 54.

4. These four lines are taken from four popular Christian songs, all of which have zoomed up the Christian music charts since the late 1990s.

5. Camerin Courtney, "O Brother, Where Art Thou?" *Christianity Today*, Single Minded. View at http://www.christianitytoday.com/singles/newsletter/mind40630.html.

Chapter 7: The Kinds of Churches Men Love

1. Mark A. Chaves, *National Congregations Study 1998* (Ann Arbor, MI: Interuniversity Consortium for Political and Social Research, 2002).

2. Chaves, *National Congregations Study 1998.*

3. Randolph E. Schmid, "US Has More Science Smarts, for the Most Part," Associated Press, as printed in *USA Today,* 19 February 2007.

4. This trend has been observed since the early 1970s in American Christianity. For more information, read Dean M. Kelley's *Why Conservative Churches Are Growing* (Mercer University Press, 1995).

5. Chaves, *National Congregations Study 1998.* The study finds a gender gap in 57.9 percent of churches that characterize themselves as "More Conservative," 67.8 percent of churches that are "Right in Middle," and 72.4 percent of churches that identify themselves as "More Liberal."

6. C. Kirk Hadaway, *FACTs on Growth: A new look at the dynamics of growth and decline in American congregations based on the Faith Communities Today 2005 national survey of Congregations.* Hartford Institute for Religion Research, http://hirr.hartsem.edu.

7. Chaves, *National Congregations Study 1998.* The study finds 60.2 percent of congregations whose senior pastor/leader was male had a gender gap, while 80.4 percent of female-led congregations had one.

8. Jawanza Kunjufu, *Adam! Where Are You?: Why Most Black Men Don't Go to Church* (Chicago: African American Images, 1997), 94.

9. Barna Research Online, "New Book and Diagnostic Resource Strive to Clear Up Widespread Confusion Regarding Leadership," 5 August 2002, www.barna.org.

Chapter 8: How to "Man Up" a Worship Service (without Driving Women Away)

1. Barbara Brown Zikmund, Adair T. Lummis, Patricia M. Y. Chang, "Women, Men and Styles of Clergy Leadership," *Christian Century,* 6 May 1998, 115, no. 14, excerpted from *Clergywomen: An Uphill Calling* (Louisville: Westminster John Knox Press, 1998).

2. Andrew Sullivan, "The He Hormone," *New York Times,* 2 April 2000. Sullivan says, "Actors tend to have more testosterone than ministers, according to a 1990 study."

Chapter 9: Men Can Learn—Really!

1. Thom and Joani Schultz, *Why Nobody Learns Much of Anything in Church: And How to Fix It* (Loveland, CO: Group, 1996), 241.

2. B. Boylan, *What's Your Point?* (New York: Warner Books, 1988), 80.

3. John Hull, *What Prevents Christian Adults from Learning?* (Philadelphia: Trinity Press International, 1991), 65.

4. Telephone interview with Pastor Dave Ferguson, 4 April 2007.

Chapter 10: How to Get James Bond to Go to Church

1. Thom S. Rainer, *Surprising Insights from the Unchurched and Proven Ways to Reach Them* (Grand Rapids: Zondervan, 2001), 111.

2. Vicki Marsh Kabat, "Old Time Religion . . . Is It Good Enough for You?" *Baylor Magazine*, January/February 2003, 19.

Chapter 11: The Mystery of Male Bonding

1. Albert L. Winseman, "Religion and Gender: A Congregation Divided, Part II," 10 December 2002. Gallup Tuesday Briefing, Religion and Values Content Channel, www.gallup.com.

2. Audrey Barrick, "Study: Men Lack Church Support," *Christian Post*, 20 Sept. 2007, posted at christianpost.com. 86 percent were every-Sunday churchgoers.

3. Robert Lewis's Men's Fraternity video series includes *The Quest for Authentic Manhood, Winning at Work and Home*, and *The Great Adventure* (Nashville: LifeWay Church Resources, 2005). For more information about how your church can use these resources, go to www.mensfraternity.com.

4. For more information about Steve Sonderman and his *Top Gun* curriculum, see www.topgunministries.com.

5. George Barna, *The Second Coming of the Church* (Nashville: Word, 1998), 2.

Chapter 12: How One Woman Can Awaken Her Congregation

1. Reprinted from *When He Doesn't Believe: Help and Encouragement for Women Who Feel Alone in Their Faith*. Copyright © 2001 by Nancy Kennedy. Waterbrook Press, Colorado Springs, CO. All rights reserved.

2. Ibid., 189.

3. Thom S. Rainer, *Surprising Insights from the Unchurched and Proven Ways to Reach Them* (Grand Rapids: Zondervan, 2001), 70.

4. Dave Barry, *Dave Barry's Complete Guide to Guys* (New York: Ballantine, 2000).

Chapter 13: What You Do . . . What God Does

1. Linda Davis, *How to Be the Happy Wife of an Unsaved Husband* (New Kensington, PA: Whitaker House, 1987), 13.

2. See Paul C. Vitz, *Faith of the Fatherless: The Psychology of Atheism* (Dallas: Spence, 1999).

3. Gary Smalley and John Trent, *The Blessing* (Nashville: Thomas Nelson, rev. ed. 2004).

Chapter 14: How We Get God off His Holy Duff

1. John Wesley, quote accessed at http://www.lifeandlibertyministries.com/archives/000243.php.

Chapter 15: Your Words Whisper; Your Life Shouts

1. Robert T. Michael, et al., *Sex in America* (Boston: Little, Brown and Co., 1994), 129.

2. Bill Hybels, Willow Creek Association Contagious Evangelism Conference, session 4, Atlanta (June 23, 2001), edited for clarity; quoted in Lee and Leslie Strobel, *Surviving a Spiritual Mismatch in Marriage* (Grand Rapids: Zondervan, 2002), 130; emphasis in original.

3. Strobel, *Surviving a Spiritual Mismatch in Marriage*, 130.

4. Reprinted from *When He Doesn't Beleve: Help and Encouragement for Women Who Feel Alone in Their Faith.* Copyright © 2001 by Nancy Kennedy. Waterbrook Press, Colorado Springs, CO. All rights reserved.

5. These lines are from a popular Christian women's book. It is written by a dear saint I personally know and love. She said I could quote her, but she would prefer to remain anonymous.

Chapter 16: How to Talk to Men about God

1. Linda Davis, *How to Be the Happy Wife of an Unsaved Husband* (New Kensington, PA: Whitaker House, 1987), 54–55.

Chapter 17: How to Lead Boys to Faith

1. Eric Young, "John Stott Announces Retirement," *The Christian Post*, 30 April 2007. Posted at http://www.christianpost.com/article/20070430/27162_ John_Stott_Announces_Retirement.htm, accessed 24 September 2007.

2. Robbie Low, "The Truth about Men & Church," *Touchstone*, June 2003, http://touchstonemag.com/archives/article.php?id=16-05-024-v.

3. "LifeWay Research Uncovers Reasons 18 to 22 Year Olds Drop Out of Church," PowerPoint presentation accompanying study, available at the LifeWay Web site, http://www.lifeway.com/lwc/article_main_page /0,1703,A=165949&M=200906,00.html, accessed 12 September 2007.

4. Paul Hill, David Anderson, and Roland Martinson, *Coming of Age: Exploring the Spirituality and Identity of Younger Men* (Minneapolis: Augsburg, 2006), 39.

5. Paul Coughlin, *No More Christian Nice Guy: When Being Nice—Instead of Good—Hurts Men, Women and Children* (Minneapolis: Bethany House, 2005), 210.

6. See, for example, *Revolve 2007: The Complete New Testament* (Nashville: Thomas Nelson, 2006); and *Refuel 2: The Complete New Testament* (Nashville: Thomas Nelson, 2nd rev. ed. 2006).

Chapter 18: Reaching All Those Other Guys (Who Don't Live Under Your Roof)

1. Lee and Leslie Strobel, *Surviving a Spiritual Mismatch in Marriage* (Grand Rapids: Zondervan, 2002), 199.

2. Ibid., 199–204.

Chapter 19: How to Support a Man in His Walk with God

1. Jeri Odell, *Spiritually Single: Living with an Unbelieving Husband* (Kansas City: Beacon Hill, 2002), 121–27.

2. David W. Augsburger, *Caring Enough to Confront: How to Understand and Express Your Deepest Feelings Toward Others,* (Ventura, CA: Regal, 1980), 9.

3. Pastor Dan Jarrell, sermon 19 March 2006, Anchorage, Alaska.

4. Larry Keefauver, *Lord, I Wish My Husband Would Pray with Me* (Lake Mary, FL: Charisma House, 1998), page xi, introduction.

5. Drs. Les and Leslie Parrott, *Saving Your Second Marriage Before It Starts: Nine Questions to Ask Before You Remarry* (Grand Rapids: Zondervan, 2001), 176.

6. Dan Schaeffer, director of Building Brothers men's ministry, frequently makes this point in his talks. Visit him at www.buildingbrothers.org.

7. Gary Chapman, *The Five Love Languages: How to Express Heartfelt Commitment to Your Mate* (Chicago: Northfield, 1995).

Chapter 20: Your Mission . . . Should You Decide to Accept It

1. Paul Coughlin, *No More Christian Nice Guy: When Being Nice—Instead of Good—Hurts Men, Women and Children* (Minneapolis: Bethany House, 2005), 59.

2. John Eldredge, interview with author, Chitina, Alaska, 31 July 2003.

ABOUT THE AUTHOR

David Murrow is not a pastor, professor, or theologian. He is just a guy in the pews who is tired of seeing churches blow it with men. He is the director of Church for Men, an organization that helps congregations reconnect with the world's largest unreached people group. His first book, *Why Men Hate Going to Church*, was an instant Christian best seller, with some one hundred thousand copies in print. His efforts have spawned articles in the *New York Times, Wall Street Journal*, and the *Chicago Tribune*, to name a few. You may have seen him on PBS, *NBC Nightly News*, or the Fox News Channel, talking about the gender gap. He lives in Alaska with his wife, three children, and a dachshund named Pepper.